The Complete DADGAD

Published by **www.fundamental-changes.com**

ISBN: 978-1-911267-09-6

Copyright © 2016 Simon Pratt

The moral right of this author has been asserted.

All rights reserved. No part of this publication may be reproduced, stored in a retrieval system, or transmitted in any form or by any means, without the prior permission in writing from the publisher. The publisher is not responsible for websites (or their content) that are not owned by the publisher.

www.fundamental-changes.com

A special Thanks to Neale McGinn for providing the tracks '4 For Blues' and 'One Day'.

'4 For Blues' and 'One Day' © Neale McGinn

Cover Image Copyright Shutterstock: Brian A Jackson

Other Books from Fundamental Changes

Contents

Get the Audio

The audio files for this book are available to download for free from **www.fundamental-changes.com** and the link is in the top right corner of the site. Simply select this book title from the drop-down menu and follow the instructions to get the audio.

We recommend that you download the files directly to your computer, not to your tablet, and extract them there before adding them to your media library. You can then put them on your tablet, iPod or burn them to CD. There is a help PDF on the download page, and we provide technical support via the contact form.

Kindle / eReaders

To get the most out of this book, remember that you can double tap any image to enlarge it. Turn off 'column viewing' and hold your kindle in landscape mode.

Twitter: @guitar_joseph
Over 5500 fans on Facebook: FundamentalChangesInGuitar
Instagram: FundamentalChanges

For over 250 Free Guitar Lessons with Videos Check Out
www.fundamental-changes.com

Introduction

The versatility of the guitar is simply incredible. While most types of music are created and played in standard EADGBE tuning, there are many popular alternatives. This book explores the fascinating world of another versatile tuning; DADGAD.

DADGAD tuning makes the guitar sound like a completely different instrument. Although we have only changed three strings from standard tuning, the difference, as you will see throughout this book, is enormous. The ringing sound created from harp-like scales and the richness and texture of even simple open chords are just two musical benefits that DADGAD can provide.

DADGAD tuning dates back to the 1960's where British folk innovator Davey Graham is widely regarded as pioneering the sound. He 'created' the tuning to inject elements of blues, jazz, and North African sounds into his Celtic music. Since then its popularity has exploded, with guitarists like Pierre Bensusan, Bert Jansch, Martin Simpson, Jimmy Page and Andy Mckee, extending Graham's early work and bringing the tuning to the masses. In fact, DADGAD is often referred to as the 'Bensusan tuning' due to his extensive use of the tuning throughout his illustrious career.

Before we dive any deeper, I want your ears to become aware of the sound that DADGAD can produce. Listen to the three tracks shown below.

Andy Mckee – Drifting
Pierre Bensusan – So Long Michael
Led Zeppelin - Kashmire

These three, different-sounding tracks give you a small glimpse into what can be achieved with DADGAD. From folk to acoustic rock, Celtic to blues and even jazz, there is something for everyone here.

If you are new to DADGAD, I recommend working your way through the book from start to finish, that way you will learn and develop techniques and skills in a logical fashion. If you are already adept at DADGAD and are just looking for new fresh ideas, then feel free to dive into any chapter you wish!

Although highly suited to acoustic guitar playing, DADGAD also works well on solid body. It can provide a valuable tool to help bust out of any ruts you may have been in, and provide a new challenge for anyone seeking to gain new guitar skills and knowledge.

Something I am so pleased about is that two of the full pieces included in this book, 'One Day', and '4 For Blues', are written by my close friend and DADGAD aficionado, Neale McGinn. They are beautiful solo acoustic guitar arrangements that you can come back to year after year. I have also written two pieces myself, 'Gone Pickin' and 'Sasha' which contain contrasting tricks and techniques using DADGAD tuning.

The audio for this book is available from **http://www.fundamental-changes.com/download-audio** so you can hear how I play and *phrase* each example.

Happy Playing!

Simon

How To Tune to DADGAD

Before you dive into all the content in this book, it is important to understand how to tune to DADGAD. Let's examine the table below.

String	Standard Tuning	DADGAD
6 (Thickest)	E	D
5	**A**	**A**
4	**D**	**D**
3	**G**	**G**
2	B	A
1 (Thinnest)	E	D

In DADGAD tuning the 5th, 4th, and 3rd strings remain identical to standard tuning EADGBE, so require no adjustment. The 6th, 2nd, and 1st strings are all tuned done one tone (two frets) *lower* than standard tuning. They need to be lowered and accurately pitched using a tuner.

If you don't have a tuner to hand, tune your 6th and 1st strings to be the same note (in different octaves) as the 4th string 'D', and the 2nd string to be the same as the 5th string 'A' an octave apart. I've made a quick video tutorial for tuning to DADGAD. You can see it here.

http://www.fundamental-changes.com/tune-dadgad-video-guitar-lesson/

Example A gives you the DADGAD tuning notes in order from the 6th (thickest) to the 1st (thinnest) string.

Example A – DADGAD Tuning Notes

A quick way to check you are in tune is to use fretted adjacent strings, similar to the '5th fret' method you may know from standard tuning. Obviously this need a little adjustment to tune to DADGAD. Example B demonstrates how to use fretted notes on adjacent strings to tune to DADGAD.

Example B – Matching Pitches

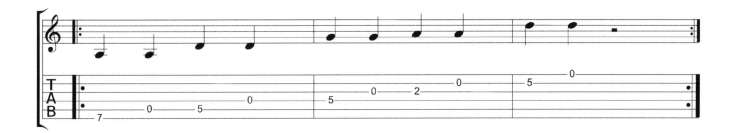

Natural harmonics are a useful tool to use for tuning (see Chapter seven for details). Example C is how I tune up using natural harmonics in DADGAD.

Example C – Tuning With Natural Harmonics

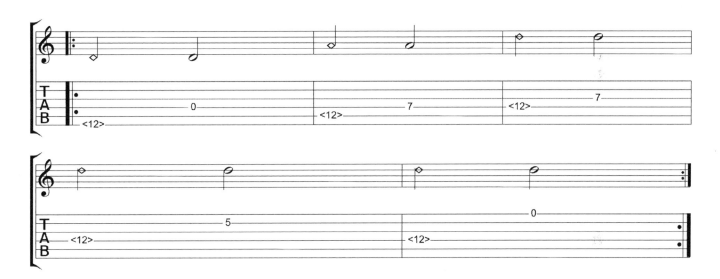

For a quick video reference guide of how to tune to DADGAD, check out this video I recorded for the Fundamental Changes website. **http://www.fundamental-changes.com/tune-dadgad-video-guitar-lesson/**

Tuning to DADGAD is much easier to understand by watching the video. You can also find it on **www.fundamental-changes.com** with the handy search function.

Chapter One – Open Chord Shapes

In this chapter, we will investigate some fundamental open chord shapes and their applications. Open chords (chords that contain open strings) are a great place to start when learning DADGAD. Although you are likely to know many open chords in standard tuning, the way you fret them in DADGAD is different. Open chords also sound different in DADGAD as they have a rich, ringing quality which is one of the defining characteristics of this wonderful tuning.

DADGAD specifically favours chords that built around a root of D, so you will notice throughout this chapter and most of the book that the chords, scales, and pieces are often written in D major or D minor.

As you work through this chapter, try to relate the new chord shapes and patterns to songs and pieces you already know. Strumming along with your favourite tunes will help you learn these chord shapes in a practical and musical way. I have included suggestions of songs you can play along to throughout the chapter.

Example 1a is a one finger chord shape. This D5 chord shape demonstrates the ringing quality of DADGAD and can be used to replace either a D major or D minor chord.

Example 1a - D5 Chord Shape

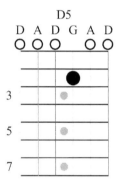

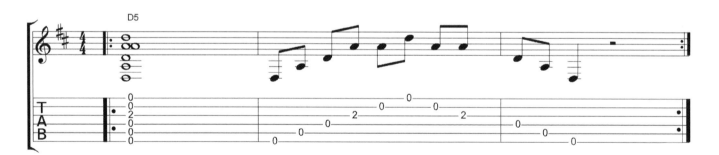

The next example is an open G chord with a 'D' as the bass note. As well as strumming the chord once and picking through each note, aim to add a simple strumming pattern to each of the chords you are learning.

Example 1b - G Chord Shape

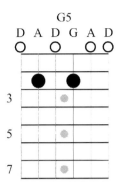

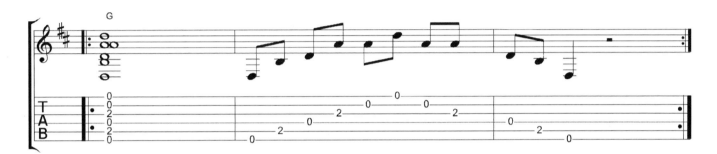

The next open chord is an open A5 shape. This shape can be used to replace an A major or A minor chord.

Example 1c – A5 Chord Shape

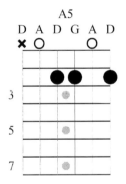

Example 1d puts the D5, G and A5 chord shapes together in a neat, two-bar strumming pattern.

Example 1d – D5 G A5

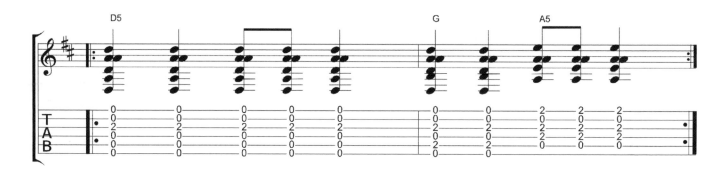

Now that you have learnt D5, G and A, here are a few songs you can strum along to using just those chords. Some of these songs may use a variety of chord shapes but for now just use the simple shapes you have learnt.

Song Name (Band)	Chords Used
Jane Says (Jane's Addiction)	G A
Bad Moon Rising (Creedence Clearwater Revival)	D G A
Free Fallin' (Tom Petty / John Mayer)	D G A
Get Back (The Beatles)	A G D

As DADGAD favours chords in the key of D, it is important to learn a variety of chord voicings that suit this tuning. This example shows two different shapes of D major.

Example 1e - D Major In Two Shapes

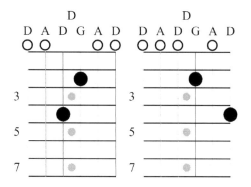

By combining strumming and picking with some beautiful open chord voicings, we can create interesting sounding rhythm guitar parts.

Example 1f – D Major To A5

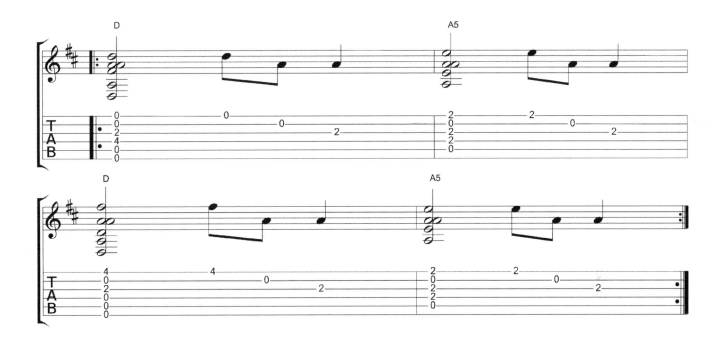

Example 1g introduces the chord of D minor in two different shapes. The darker, sadder tones of minor chords played in DADGAD tuning are a personal favourite.

As you go through this book, I recommend highlighting your preferred shapes, that way you can concentrate on really 'nailing' those chords and have them ready for future use.

Example 1g – D Minor In Two Shapes

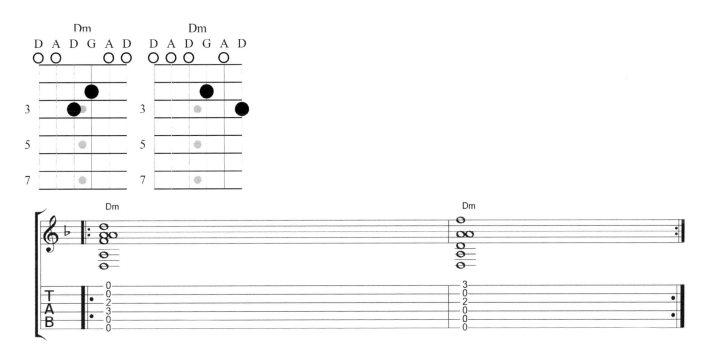

Example 1h uses the same rhythmic template laid out in example 1f but includes the D minor chord voicings instead of the D major shapes.

Example 1h – D Minor To A5

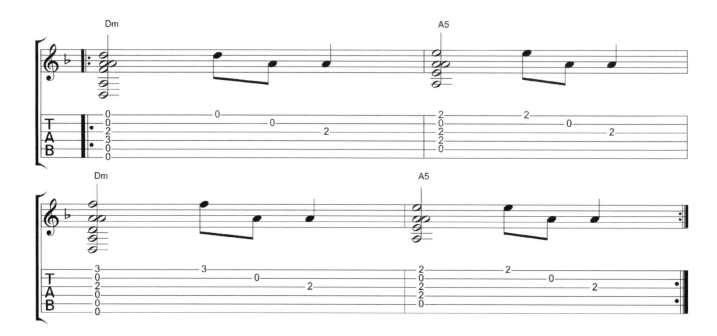

Here are two more useful open DADGAD chord voicings to learn, C major and A minor.

Example 1i – C Major and A Minor Chords

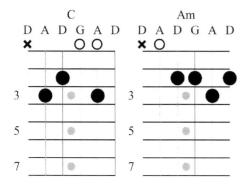

In example 1j I create a picked arpeggio pattern around the C major and A minor chord shapes.

Example 1j – Picking C Major and A Minor

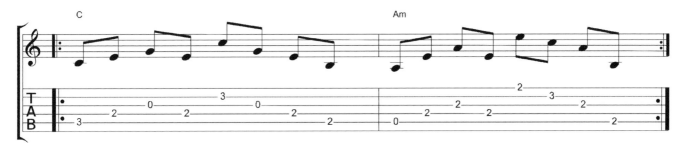

Example 1k adds the note 'E' on the thinnest string to create a fuller-sounding C major chord voicing.

Example 1k – C Major Full Voicing

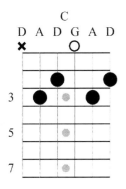

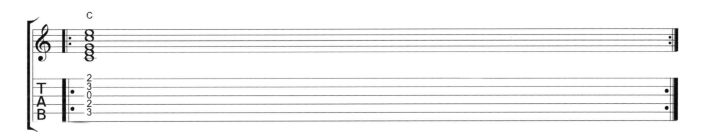

Here in example 1l, I have created a simple yet effective rhythmic pattern. The addition of the strummed mute, notated as X's adds a percussive element to this chord sequence. Don't worry if the C major and A minor shapes still feel a little more uncomfortable than the D minor; that is because they are four finger shapes and require a bit more practice.

Example 1l – D Minor Chord Progression

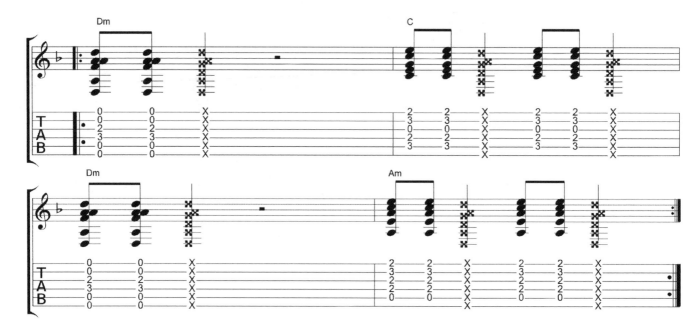

Example 1m demonstrates one of the most powerful techniques you can use with DADGAD chord shapes. By moving a power chord shape on the lower strings while the higher strings are ringing we can create different chords. Here I have shown four of the most common places you can apply the shape, but please feel free to experiment with other frets and see how they sound.

You can either barre the notes with one finger, or you can use different fingers to fret each note. I use a first finger barre to create these 'mini chords' as it is easier to move around than separate fingers.

Example 1m – Mini Barre Chord Shapes

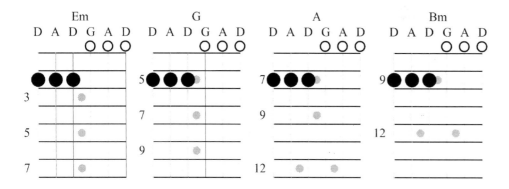

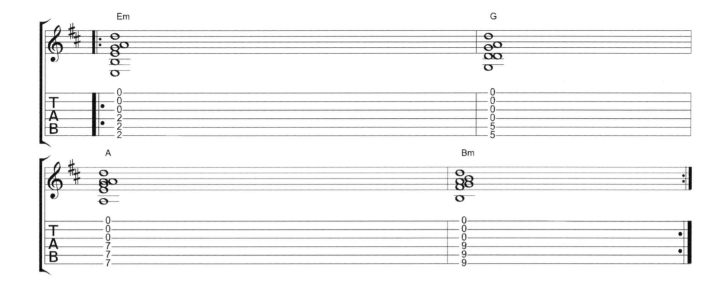

In the next example, I combine an open D major voicing with the G and A chord shapes from the previous example. Feel free to create your own strumming, picking or finger picking patterns with any of the chords seen in this chapter.

Example 1n – Ringing Chords

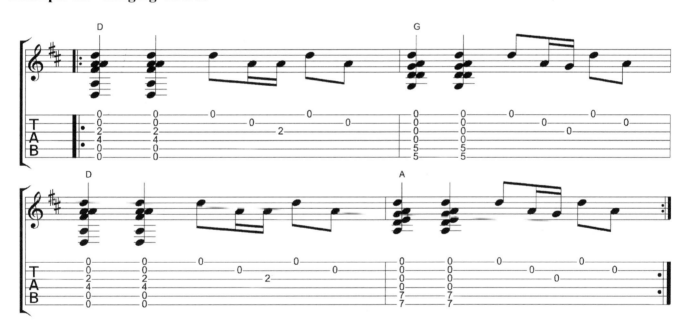

Example 1o shows one of the most commonly used chord progressions in pop music. For an incredible video that demonstrates this, check out The Axis of Awesome's video called 4 chords.

https://www.youtube.com/watch?v=5pidokakU4I

Example 1o – Pop Chord Progression

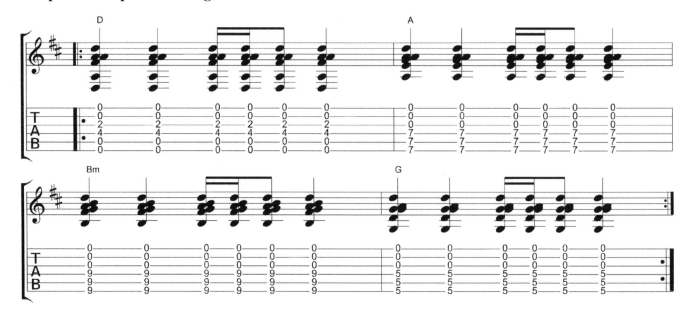

Here are the chords seen in the previous example but with a slightly different shape and sound.

Example 1p – Pop Pattern Part 2

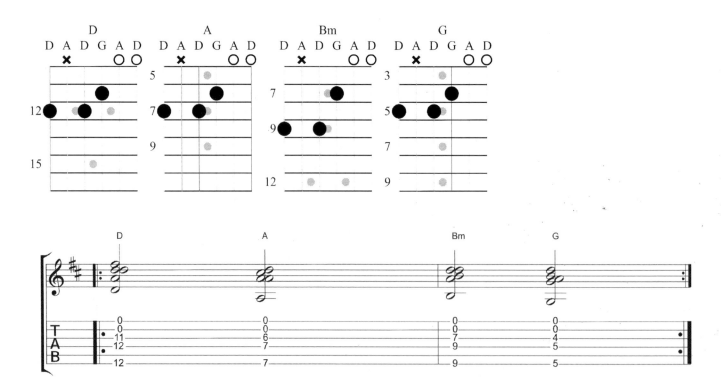

By picking each note individually, you can hear the sound of the chord and check to see if there are any muffled notes.

Example 1q – Picked Chords

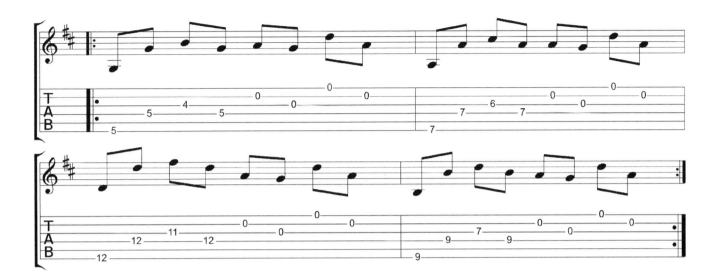

The symbol 'D/F#' simply means a D major chord with an F# as the bass note. This chord is a common passing chord and a very popular sound in this tuning.

Example 1r – D/F# Chord Shape

The following piece, 'Picky' centres on the use of open chord shapes. All the chords used in this track will feel familiar to you, as you have learnt them throughout this opening chapter.

Using A Metronome

When you are learning any of the DADGAD pieces or examples featured in this book, always use a metronome.

Begin playing each example very slowly with the metronome set at 50bpm, and make sure that every note is clean and audible.

When you can play an example perfectly three times in a row at 50bpm, raise the metronome up to 53bpm. Continue to increase the metronome speed in increments of 3 beats-per-minute up to your target speed of 80bpm+. This form of structured practice means that you will only increase your speed once the example is played accuratcly.

I use the Tempo app (made by Frozen Ape) on my phone, as I know I will always have my phone with me and I'll never have an excuse practice without a metronome. **Example 1s – Picky**

Chapter Two – Open String Scales

In this chapter, we will explore useful DADGAD open scales. By learning a scale with a lick attached to it, you will be able to see how to use each scale in a musical context. Open string scales and licks work particularly well in Blues, Country, and Folk music but can be applied to any genre.

The scales you will learn in the chapter are:

- D Major Scale
- D Minor Pentatonic Scale
- D Blues Scale
- D Mixolydian Scale

As well as learning the licks I have provided, I highly recommend creating your own ideas using each of the scales in this chapter.

Example 2a shows the open D Major scale (D E F# G A B C#) across all six strings. When learning these scales watch your picking hand and make sure you are applying strict 'down, up' alternate picking.

Example 2a – D Major Scale

In example 2b, I created a simple melodic theme using the open D Major scale. The ringing sound that can be achieved in DADGAD is shown here, by playing multiple open strings in a row.

Example 2b – D Major Scale Lick 1

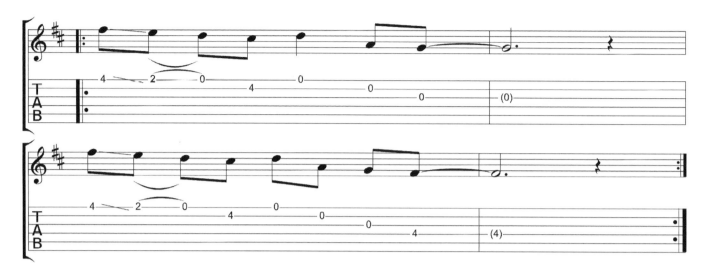

A powerful technique to use in DADGAD is to have a droning string ring underneath melodic phrases. In example 2c, I let the open sixth string note of 'D' ring out while I play a simple folk style theme on the top.

Be sure to listen to the recorded audio files of every example in this book to hear the nuance of how I play the licks.

You can get your audio files here:

http://www.fundamental-changes.com/download-audio/

Example 2c – D Major Scale Lick 2

Now we have learnt the open D Major scale, it is time to learn the D Minor Pentatonic scale (D F G A C).

Example 2d – D Minor Pentatonic

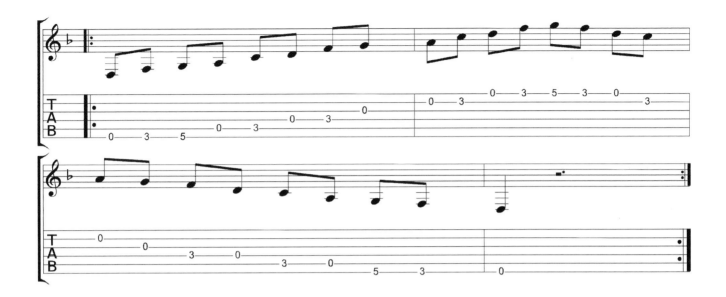

Example 2e has a raw acoustic blues feel and uses mini blues 'curls' to add expression to the notes. A 'curl' is the smallest audible distance you can bend a string on the guitar. Listen out to the difference between the muted notes (labeled P.M.) and the ordinary fretted notes in the accompanying audio.

Example 2e – D Minor Pentatonic Lick 1

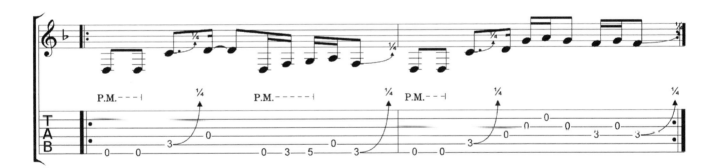

Example 2f uses the open D Minor Pentatonic scale and a *call and response* phrase. At the end of bars two and four we have some power chord shapes. These will be explained in more detail in a later chapter.

Example 2f – D Minor Pentatonic Lick 2

Now let's learn the open D Blues scale (D F G Ab A C) which adds one new note 'Ab' to the D Minor Pentatonic scale.

Example 2g – D Blues Scale

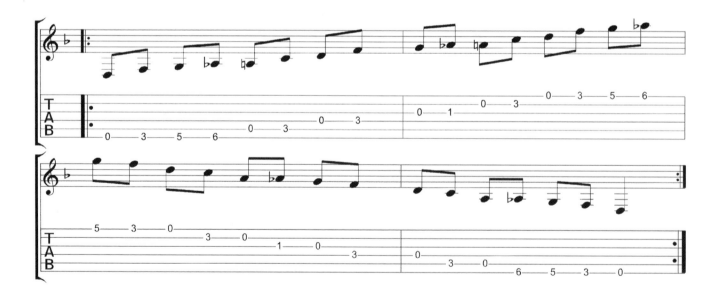

Example 2h acts as a primer for the mini piece 'Stevie goes to DADGAD that follows this example. The extra time spent learning this primer will help you to play "Stevie goes to DADGAD" far more quickly.

Work on this lick slowly at first with a metronome at around 60 beats per minute and make sure every note is clear and audible. Only when you feel completely comfortable playing it at this speed should you consider raising the tempo.

Example 2h – D Blues Scale Lick

Example 2i – Stevie Goes to DADGAD

Stevie Goes To DADGAD is a mini tribute to the unbelievable talent of Stevie Ray Vaughan. I used example 2h as the theme to an entire twelve-bar blues progression. By alternating between a single note picking lick and strummed chords, Stevie Goes To DADGAD combines both rhythm and lead guitar. This piece sounds great at any tempo, but when you speed it up it is a real show stopper.

Stevie Goes to DADGAD

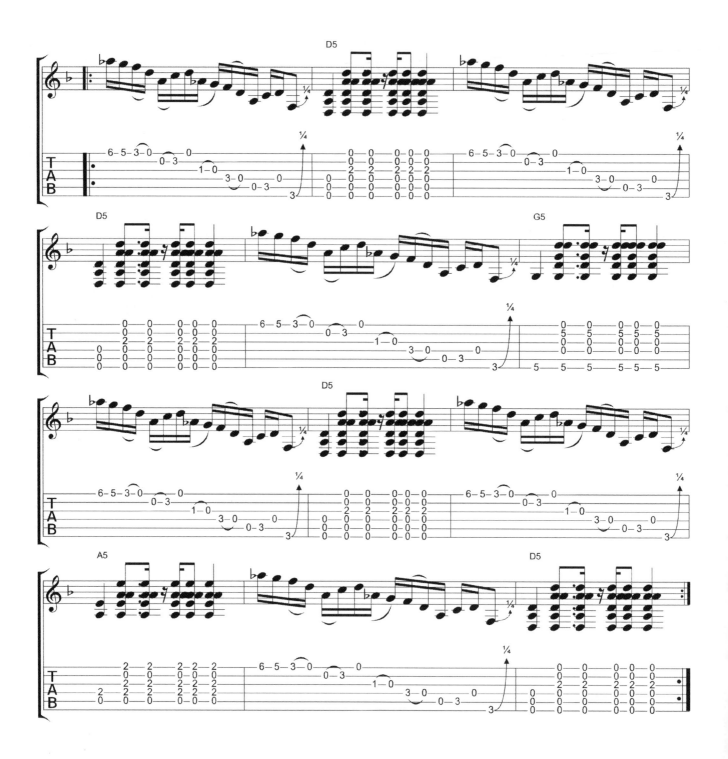

The final open scale in this chapter is D Mixolydian (D E F# G A B C). This scale works brilliantly over D7 chords.

Example 2j – D Mixolydian Scale

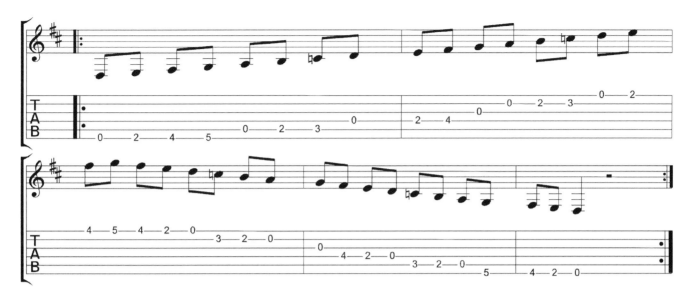

Example 2k has a John Mayer sound and combines an open D7 chord with two different D Mixolydian licks.

Example 2k – John Mayer DADGAD Lick

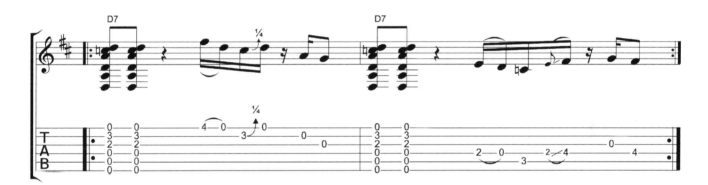

The ringing quality of the open string scale allows for some nice variations, instead of always playing fretted note scales. The examples featured throughout this chapter are all using the root note of 'D', but as you progress further in your DADGAD journey you can learn other open string DADGAD scales in a wider variety of keys.

Keep in mind that open string scales cannot be easily moved, but if you love the sound of a particular open string DADGAD scale and want to play it in a different key, you can always use a capo.

Chapter Three – Twelve-Bar Blues

Now that you have mastered open chords and scales it's time to look at one of the most important and popular music structures in music. From Status Quo to Chuck Berry… The Rolling Stones to Led Zeppelin: almost all rock and pop musicians have used the twelve-bar blues form to write songs.

The twelve-bar blues is a brilliant structure to play, either on your own or with other musicians. In this chapter, I am going to show you how to play a twelve-bar blues progression using DADGAD tuning. The rhythm that is commonly used alongside the twelve-bar blues is a 'shuffle' rhythm. Lazily say the phrase 'chunka-chunka' and you will get a good idea of how this should sound.

I highly recommend that as you go through this chapter, you jam with a friend or, indeed, by yourself using a looping device or through recording yourself.

Example 3a demonstrates the basic two-bar building block of the twelve-bar blues. I recommend using all down picks when playing this pattern, and to keep the pick strokes as dynamically even as possible.

Example 3a

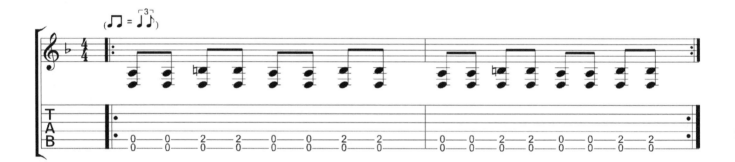

By adding in the extra note 'C' on the 'A' string we can create a common twelve-bar blues variation.

Example 3b

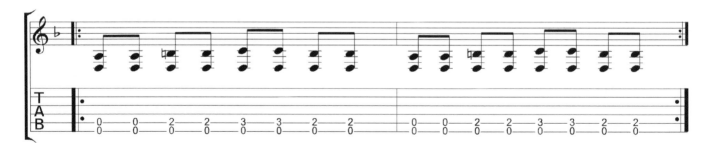

In example 3c we create a fatter sound by adding in the octave 'D' note to create a three note chord sequence.

Example 3c

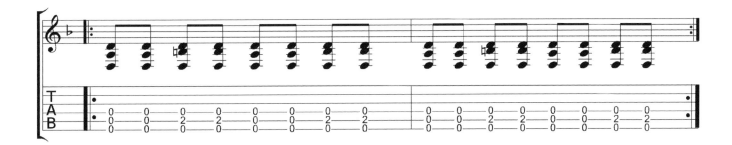

Next we can add the note 'C' to the new three-note shapes.

Example 3d

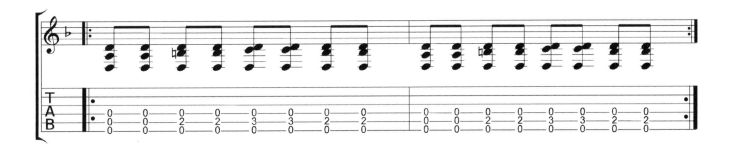

After you have mastered the open string shapes, it's time to learn the next part of the twelve-bar blues using a movable shape. Example 3a demonstrates this movable shape in 'G', which will be used for bars 5,6 and 10 of the full twelve-bar blues progression.

Example 3e

Now we have learnt the movable shape in 'G', it is easy to move it into 'A'. This pattern will be used for bars 9 and 12 in the full twelve-bar pattern in 'D'.

Example 3f

Next it is time to place all the previously learnt bars into the full twelve-bar blues pattern. This should feel comfortable if you have grasped the examples in this chapter up to this point.

As this is the foundation of the rest of the chapter, commit it to memory so you don't have to read it from the page. Also, record it into a looping device, phone or recording software so you can have it as a backing track to jam along to with the licks later on in the chapter.

Example 3g – Full Twelve-Bar Blues Foundation

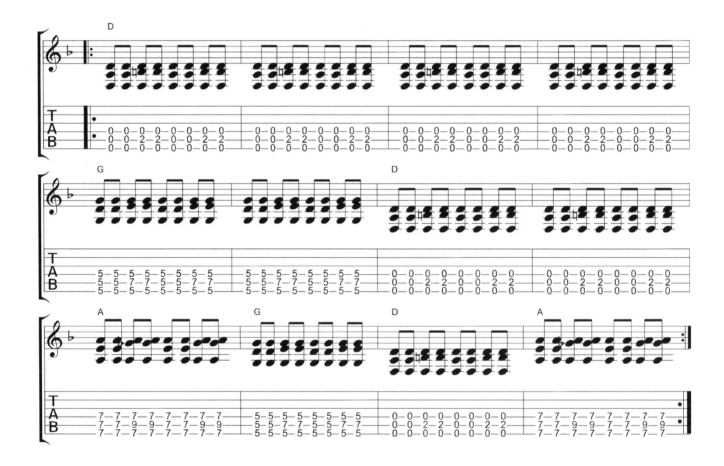

Once you have grasped example 3g you can learn a variation of the full twelve-bar blues progression. This example may feel slightly trickier on the shapes of 'G' and 'A', but stick at it is worth the extra practice.

Example 3h – Twelve-Bar Blues Variation

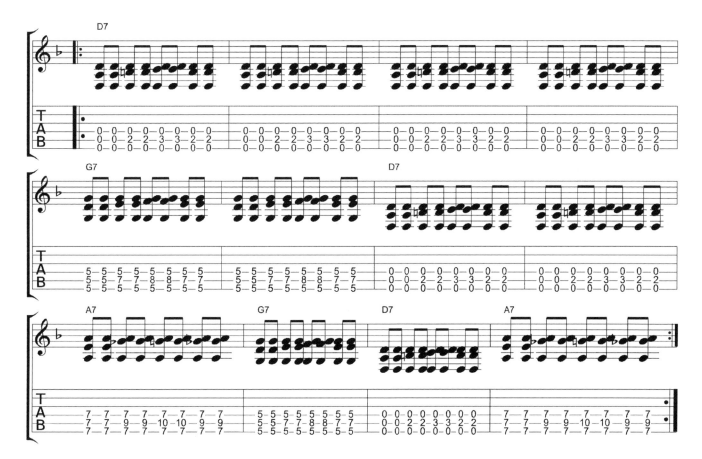

One of the first pieces I ever performed live was the song Get It On, by T-Rex. Although the main riff is simple, it is also incredibly memorable. I based example 3i on that riff by adding open strings to the previously learnt twelve-bar blues pattern. Although not notated in the music, you can let the open strings ring out between all the chords to give this twelve-bar pattern its unique sound.

Example 3i – Twelve-Bar Blues With Open Strings

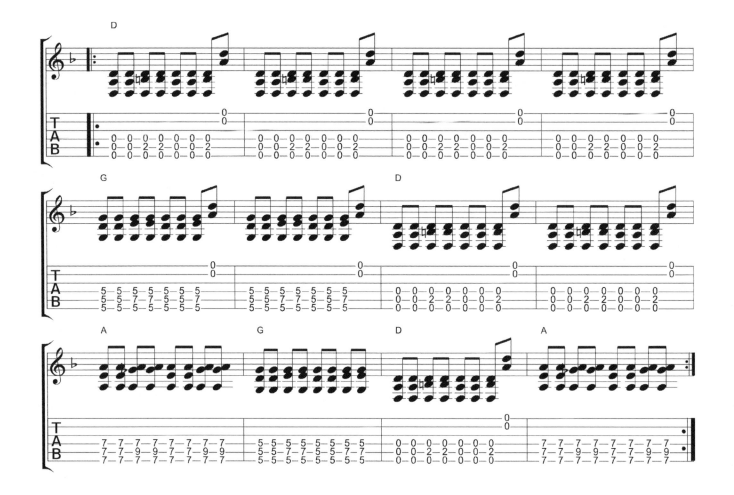

In blues guitar, it is common to use 'turnaround' licks either at the start or end (sometimes both) of twelve-bar blues progressions. A turnaround is almost always two bars long, and it is a way of 'turning you back around' so the piece can repeat from the beginnig. Any of the turnaround licks seen in this chapter can be used instead of the final two bars of a twelve-bar progression.

Example 3j – Turnaround lick 1

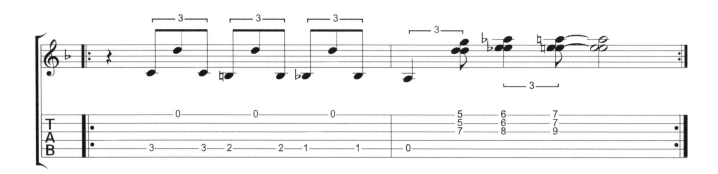

Rhythmically, turnarounds often follow a structured pattern. Often the first beat of the first bar is a rest and then a series of triplets is used to descend or ascend to the final chord. A fun easy way to count triplets is to use any three-syllable word. I prefer 'el-e-phant' but you can pick one that suits you. Put on a metronome and count out this triplet pattern to work on your rhythmic awareness as well as practicing the licks seen here.

Example 3k – Turnaround lick 2

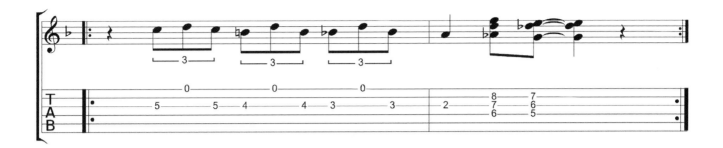

Example 3l shows a slight variation on the previous example by including the extra open string note of 'A'.

Example 3l – Turnaround lick 3

As well as picking notes individually, blues players often play multiple notes at once when playing turnarounds. For this example, you can either use fingerpicking or hybrid picking (pick and fingers) to pluck the required notes.

Example 3m – Turnaround lick 4

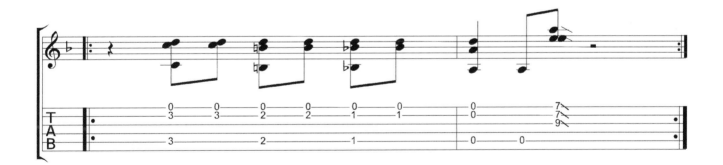

Example 3n is the fifth and final turnaround lick. I recommend that you use a pick to play this lick as it will be easier than fingerpicking. This lick shows that you can play turnaround licks higher up the neck as well as lower down.

Now that you have five different turnaround licks, you can add them to the twelve-bar blues progressions shown earlier in the chapter by replacing the final two bars of the progression.

You can then play through the twelve-bar blues progression five times and have a different ending each time. This adds interest and variation and will ultimately make it more enjoyable to play.

Example 3n- Turnaround lick 5

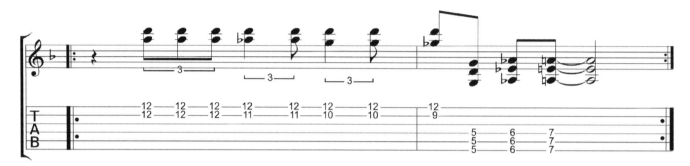

Example 3o is a twelve-bar blues pattern that alternates between picking notes and strumming the mini chords shapes. The final two bars of this progression use the turnaround phrase from example 3k.

Example 3o – Twelve Bar Blues With Turnaround

Once you are comfortable and familiar with how to build a twelve-bar blues progression you can learn some lead guitar licks that fit over the top of that pattern. Then you will be able to have a great time jamming with a friend, as one person plays the rhythm part and the other plays some lead guitar lines.

Example 3p is a bluesy line that uses the D Blues scale (D F G Ab A C). Sometimes when it comes to lead guitar the simpler the lick, the better it sounds. **Example 3p**

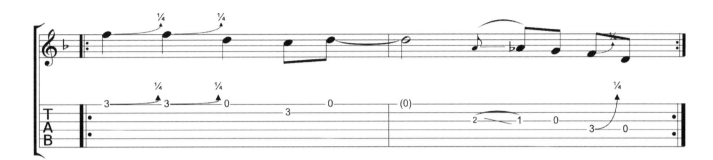

The next lick once again uses the D Blues scale with a mixture of hammer-ons, pull-offs and mini blues curls. **Example 3q**

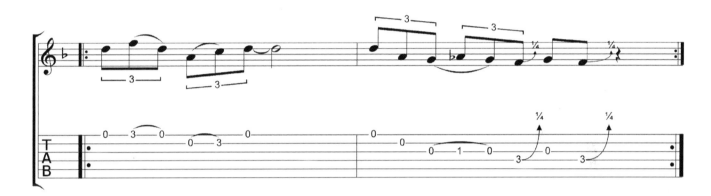

When it comes to soloing and lead guitar, I am all about making the most of what you already have. Example 3r is just example 3p up an octave, it contains the same notes and musical phrasing but will cut through a mix more due to it being higher up the fretboard.

Example 3r

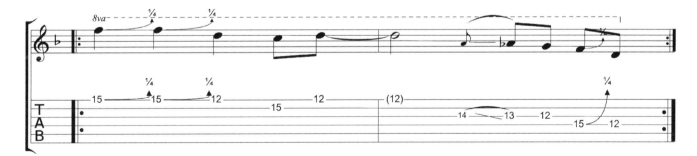

Example 3s is example 3q up an octave. Every lick that you write, make sure you can play the same lick up or down an octave from its original pitch. That way you will always get two licks for the price of one!

Example 3s

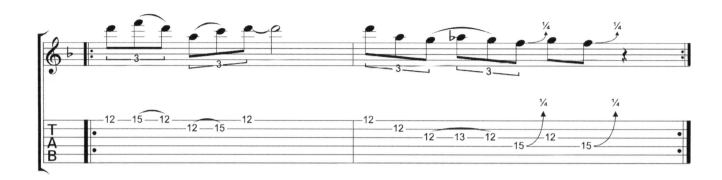

For the final example in this chapter, I have created a twelve-bar blues mini solo using the licks and a turnaround that you have learnt throughout this chapter. Have fun with it and use it as a template to create your own soloing ideas.

Example 3t

Chapter Four – Movable Chords

In chapter one we focussed on open chords and applications. Although open chords sound great, they are restrictive in that they can only be played in certain keys. In this chapter, I will show you major, minor, major 7th, minor 7th and dominant 7th movable chord voicings. You will be able to play these chords in any key allowing for the freedom to play a lot of songs. Before we start learning the voicings, it is important to remember that the fretboard notes are different to standard tuning. Let's examine the notes on the 6th string, as this will be where we name most of the chords from in this chapter.

6th String Neck Diagram in DADGAD

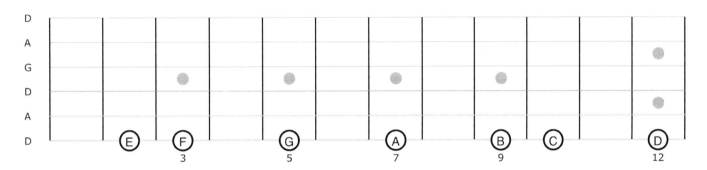

If you are familiar with the notes on the 6th string in standard tuning, it will feel new to you naming the notes in DADGAD. Just remember that everything is a tone (or two frets) lower than in standard tuning.

Example 4a shows a movable major chord voicing played from the root note of 'F'. Although this chord shape does require all four fingers, it is significantly easier than learning a major barre chord shape in standard tuning. **Example 4a**

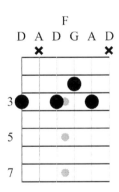

When learning a new chord shape, it is good practice to pick every note of the chord individually to see if there are any notes that are not sounding correctly. Example 4b uses the movable major chord voicing in 'F' and 'G' and picks through the notes using 1/8th notes.

Example 4b

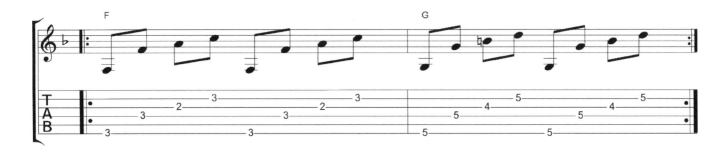

Now that the movable major chord shape feels comfortable, and each note is ringing clearly, we can apply a fingerpicking pattern to a popular chord progression. I use my picking-hand knuckles to create the slap sounds here shown by the muted notes. This percussive effect is an effective way to add percussion to rhythmic playing patterns.

Example 4c

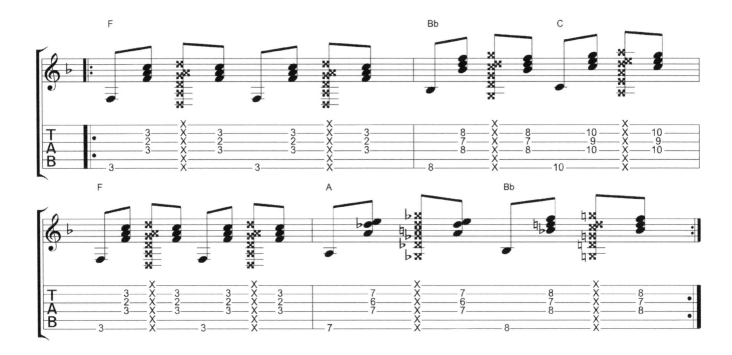

Another movable major chord voicing uses the top four strings. The root note of this voicing is on the 4th (D) string in this case 'F'.

4th String Neck Diagram in DADGAD

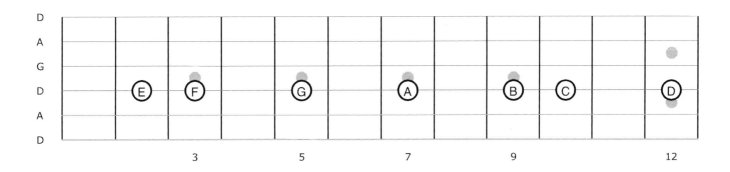

Example 4d

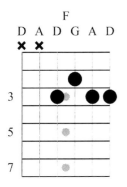

Can you name the chords shown below? They are major chords, with their root notes on the 4th string. Use the neck diagram on the previous page to find the root notes.

Example 4e

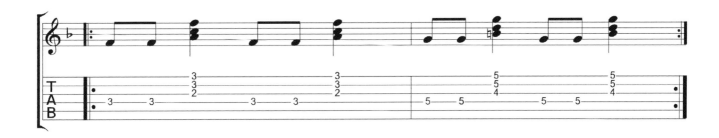

The inspiration behind the strumming pattern seen in example 4f is the song Torn, by Natalie Imbruglia. The syncopated 1/16th note pattern is a fun one to add to your rhythm guitar trick bag.

Example 4f

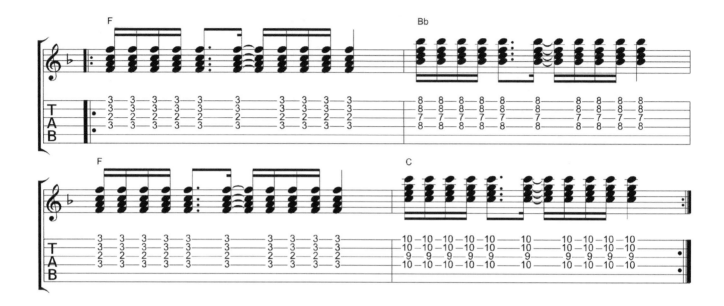

Example 4g demonstrates a movable minor shape in G minor with the root note on the 6th string.

Example 4g

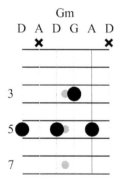

It is important when learning new chord shapes to be able to use them in chord progressions. Having a lot of chord progressions at your disposal will allow you to write music quicker and have a selection of instant 'jamming' material.

Example 4h

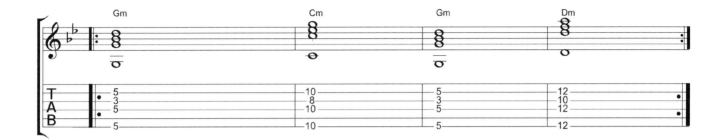

Example 4i combines movable minor and major chord shapes into a Latin-sounding picking pattern. This example can be played using a pick or with fingers, the option is yours.

Example 4i

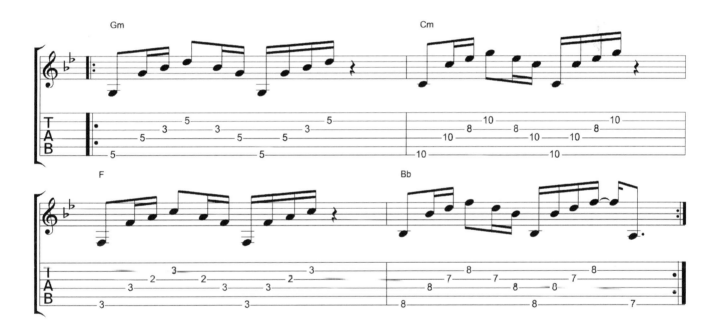

Example 4j introduces a higher-pitched movable minor chord voicing. The root note for this chord shape is on the 4th string, creating the chord of G minor in this example.

Example 4j

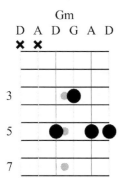

By playing on the off-beats instead of the 1 2 3 4, we can create a simple reggae groove. Count 1 + 2 + 3 + 4 + but only play on the +'s along with your metronome. (+'s are pronounced 'and' when counting).

Example 4k

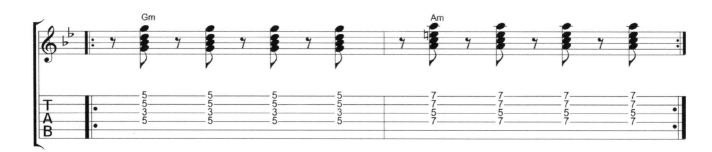

In example 4l, we split up the four-note chord by strumming the top three notes and picking the root note separately.

This idea combines both the movable minor and major shapes on the upper four strings. **Example 4l**

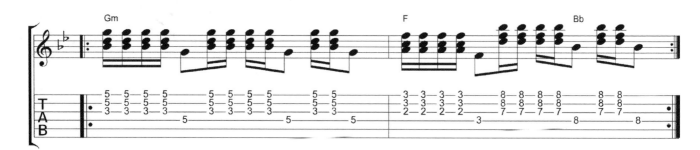

Major and minor chords form the core of everything we play, but they can often sound a little bland. Using more sophisticated voicings of major 7, minor 7 and dominant 7 very quickly adds excitement to your chordal playing.

Example 4m demonstrates a movable major 7 chord voicing with the root note on the 6th string, in this case creating a G major 7 chord. I recommend applying a barre across the 4th fret with your first finger, but alternatively, you can play each note with separate fingers if that feels more comfortable.

Example 4m

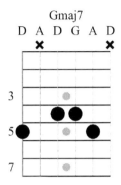

This example uses G major 7 and C major 7 to create a happy two-chord jazz progression.

Example 4n

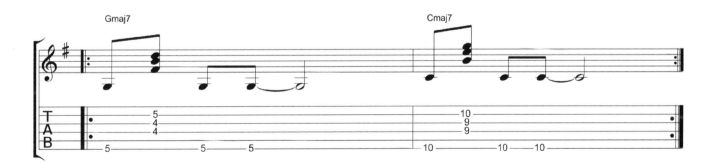

Example 4o shows a movable minor 7 chord shape, with the root note on the D string. Here at the 5th fret that creates a G minor 7 chord.

Example 4o

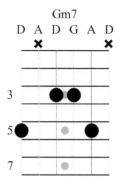

This minor 7 groove has a distinctly Latin feel to it. **Example 4p**

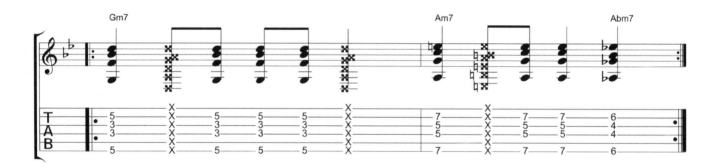

The dominant 7th chord is a foundation to all blues music. This movable shape will allow you to play a twelve-bar blues progression in any key. **Example 4q**

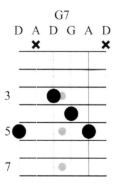

In the previous chapter, I showed you how to play a twelve-bar blues using DADGAD tuning. This next example shows you a twelve-bar blues progression but this time is in the key of 'G' and not 'D'. The great thing about example 4r is that you can take the shapes laid out here and move the whole progression to any key that you want to play in.

Example 4r

I have written a piece I have called 'Sevens' that uses all the different 7th voicings you have learnt so far. Sevens has an upbeat funky vibe to it and is in the key of D minor. The fills between the chords predominantly come from the D Blues scale.

I have purposely not given the chord symbols in the notation as I would like you to work them out using the knowledge you have gained from this chapter. Use the neck diagram to work out the root note and then you should recognise the different shapes from the previous examples.

Example 4s – Sevens

Sevens

5th String Neck Diagram in DADGAD

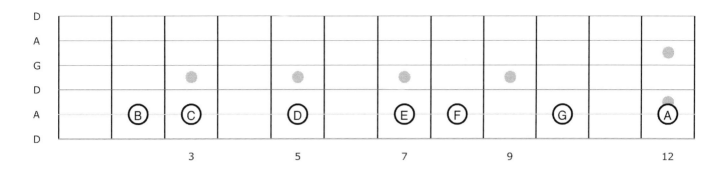

As well as learning 7th chords with a root note on the 6th string, it is useful to learn 7th chord shapes with a root on the 5th string. By using the neck diagram above you will be able to name your 5th string root 7th chords.

Example 4t shows a movable major 7 chord shape with the root note on the 5th string, in this case creating a D major 7 chord.

Example 4t

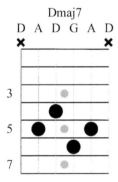

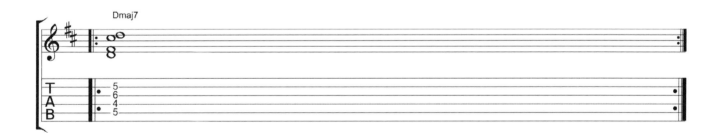

The next example is a movable minor 7 chord shape, with the root on the 5th string. At the 5th fret, this creates a D minor 7 chord.

Example 4u

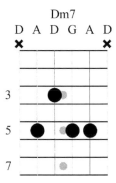

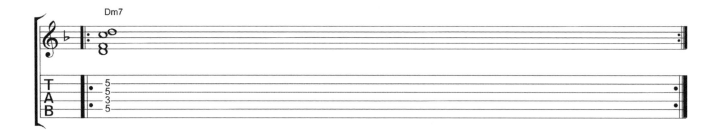

The final chord shape is a dominant 7th chord with its root on the 5th string. Example 4v demonstrates this with a D7 chord.

Example 4v

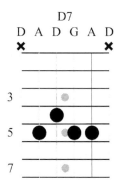

Earlier in the chapter, I showed you how to play a twelve-bar blues in the key of 'G' with movable dominant 7th shapes. The advantage of knowing chord shapes with roots on different strings is that it makes for more accessible moves between shapes.

Example 4w is a twelve-bar blues progression, this time in the key of 'A'. By combining 6th and 5th string voicings of dominant 7th chords you can see how effective knowing two shapes of the same chord type can be.

Example 4w

Now that you have completed this chapter, I urge you to put your new chord shape skills to the test. Pick a song that you already know that contains only major and minor chords (if you are stuck for ideas see below), and figure out how you can play those songs in DADGAD tuning. The more repertoire you can build in DADGAD the better, and the more fun it will be for you especially when someone asks you to "play them something".

Here are some songs you can figure out in DADGAD tuning. They use simple major and minor chord voicings. (Songs may be simplified slightly or moved to a more convenient key for DADGAD tuning).

Song Name	Chords Used
Twist and Shout – The Beatles	D G A and (A7)
Hey Ya - Outkast	G C D E
Hey Joe – Jimi Hendrix	C G D A E
Stand By Me – Ben E King	A F#m D E

Brown Eyed Girl – Van Morrison	G C D Em
Hotel California – The Eagles	Bm F# A E G D Em F#

Once you feel comfortable moving between all the major and minor chord voicings in the song list above, you can learn some songs that include major 7th, minor 7th and dominant 7th chord voicings. (Songs may be simplified slightly or moved to a more convenient key for DADGAD tuning).

Song Name	Chords Used
Something – The Beatles	C Cmaj7 C7 F D G Am C C#m F#m
Kiss Me – Sixpence None The Richer *	Eb Ebma7 Eb7 Fm Bb Cm Abmaj7
Light My Fire – The Doors *	Am7 F#m7 G A D B E F
Tune Up – Miles Davis	Em7 A7 Dmaj7 Dm7 G7 Cmaj7 Cm7 F7 Bbma7

Although slightly less common than regular major and minor chord voicings, 7th chords crop up more than you would expect. They are particularly popular in jazz and appear in almost every jazz standard.

Some of the tunes may be in slightly different keys from the original, but I have tried to keep them as close as possible while retaining accessibility within DADGAD tuning. You will need to listen to the original songs to hear where each of these chords fit. This is a fantastic opportunity for you to work on training your ear to hear where chords fit within a song. If you are struggling to do that, use a chord sheet online to follow along with the track.

*Simplified slightly

Chapter Five – Movable Scales and Arpeggio Shapes

Movable scale shapes are a fundamental skill to master when learning the guitar, regardless of the tuning. Although learning chord shapes in DADGAD can seem a little daunting, mastering movable scale shapes will feel easier if you are used to playing them in standard tuning.

Let's recap on how this tuning is constructed.

Tuning	6th	5th	4th	3rd	2nd	1st
Standard	E	**A**	**D**	**G**	B	E
DADGAD	D	**A**	**D**	**G**	A	D

Notice that the 5th, 4th and 3rd strings are identical to standard tuning (highlighted in bold) and the 6th, 2nd and 1st strings are a tone (or two frets) lower. This is <u>extremely</u> important to grasp before moving through the rest of this chapter.

The great news is that all the scale shapes you have previously learnt in standard tuning will work in DADGAD, but they will require a little re-arrangement.

Scales

Example 5a is the A Minor Pentatonic scale (A C D E G) in standard tuning. This is for reference only; you do not need to re-tune your guitar at this point.

Example 5a – A Minor Pentatonic in standard tuning

A Minor Pentatonic
E Shape

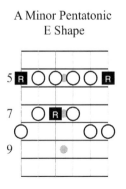

Example 5b shows the A Minor Pentatonic scale but this time in DADGAD tuning. The notes shown here are identical to the notes shown in the above example. Notice how the 6th, 2nd and 1st strings are fretted two frets above example 5a but the 5th, 4th and 3rd strings are identical.

This principle works for every scale when converting it from standard tuning to DADGAD. The notes on the 6th, 2nd and 1st strings need to be played two frets above where they are played in standard tuning, but the 5th, 4th and 3rd strings can stay the same.

This also works for any chord shape that you may know in standard tuning that uses only the 5th, 4th and 3rd strings. They will fit perfectly in DADGAD tuning as there is no change to the tuning on those strings.

Example 5b – A Minor Pentatonic in DADGAD

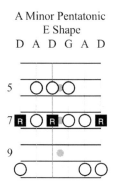

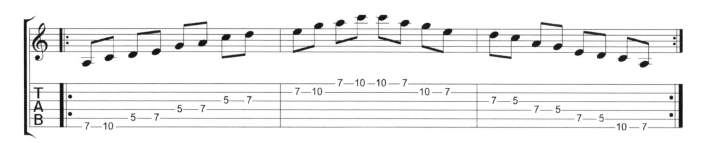

Now that you have learnt the A Minor Pentatonic scale in DADGAD tuning it is time to play some musical vocabulary in that scale. Example 5c is a classic blues lick reminiscent of early Eric Clapton.

Example 5c – A Minor Pentatonic lick

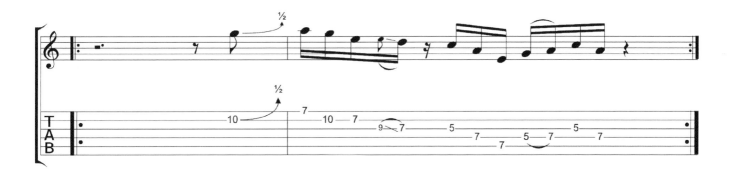

The next scale to concentrate on is the A Blues scale (A C D Eb E G). This scale is built by adding one extra note of 'Eb' to the A Minor Pentatonic scale (A C D E G).

For those of you familiar with the A Blues scale in standard tuning, it should feel very easy to adapt it to DADGAD by following the procedure mentioned above.

Example 5d – A Blues scale

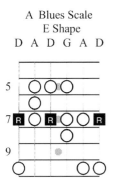

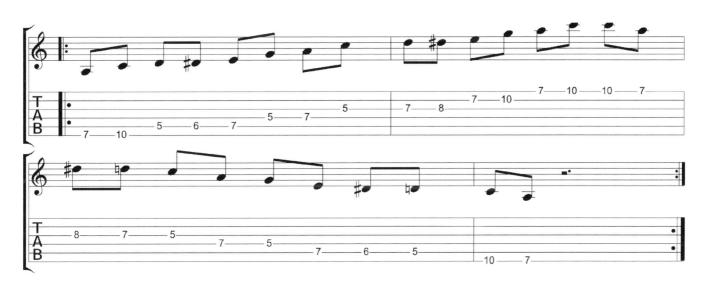

Blues players like B.B King often use mini blues 'curl' bends to add expression to a note. Example 5e demonstrates using blues 'curls' within the A Blues scale.

Example 5e – A Blues scale lick

Example 5f is the A Major Pentatonic scale (A B C# E F#). Popular in blues and country, guitar stars like Slash and Jimi Hendrix often use this scale.

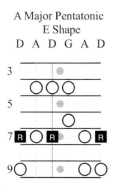

A Major Pentatonic
E Shape
D A D G A D

Example 5f

If Hendrix had tuned to DADGAD, he may have created something along the lines of Example 5g. The combination of the A Major Pentatonic scale and double stops creates a Hendrix-style DADGAD vibe.

Example 5g

Now that you have learnt the A Major Pentatonic scale in DADGAD you can learn the A Major scale (A B C# D E F# G#).

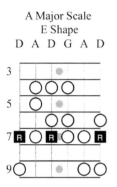

A Major Scale
E Shape
D A D G A D

Example 5h

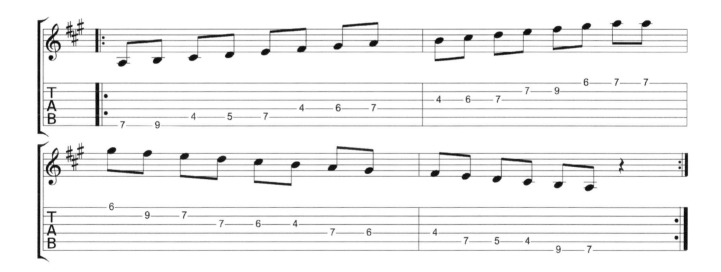

In example 5i, I created a melodic theme using the A Major scale. There are a lot of slides in this idea, so start off slowly, with a metronome, and make sure all your slides are clean and audible.

Example 5i

Here in is the A Mixolydian scale (A B C# D E F# G) in DADGAD tuning.

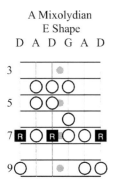

Example 5j

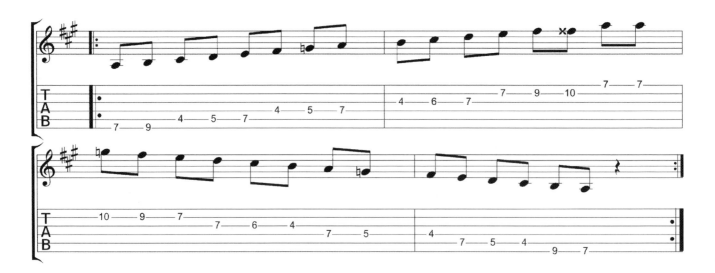

Example 5k is a syncopated A Mixolydian blues lick. Listen to the audio to see how I phrase this lick.

Example 5k

The final movable scale in this chapter is the A Natural Minor scale (A B C D E F G). Remember that you can play any of the scales featured in this chapter in any key.

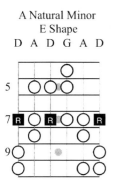

A Natural Minor
E Shape
D A D G A D

Example 5l

The Natural Minor scale has a sad, melancholic sound and is popular with classic rock guitarists like Carlos Santana. This example uses the A Natural Minor scale with slides and legato to create a DADGAD rock sound.

Remember that DADGAD works well on both an acoustic or electric guitar. Just because traditionally it has been more popular on an acoustic does not mean you have to stick to that convention.

Example 5m

Arpeggios

Now that you have studied chords and scales it is time to look at how to create arpeggios using DADGAD tuning.

An arpeggio is the notes of a chord played one at a time, sometimes referred to as a broken chord. In this chapter, I will show you how to play movable major, minor, major 7th, minor 7th and dominant 7th arpeggios (these match up with the chords you learnt in the previous chapter). Make sure you apply strict alternate picking (down, up) and use a metronome set slowly at around 60bpm when learning these shapes.

By learning the arpeggio shapes shown in this chapter you will improve your knowledge of the fretboard in DADGAD tuning. For an extra challenge, try naming the names as you play them. Refer to the appendix at the end of this book for neck diagrams of the notes in DADGAD.

Example 5n shows a C major arpeggio (C E G). You will notice that there is no note played on the 'G' string. This is because of the nature of DADGAD tuning, and would cause a repetition of the same note.

Example 5n – C Major Arpeggio

All the arpeggios shown in this chapter are movable and it is fun to create technique-builder exercises to aid fretboard fluency. Example 5o moves the major arpeggio through multiple keys of C, Eb and G.

Example 5o – Major Arpeggio Exercise

Example 5p is a movable minor arpeggio shape in the key of C minor (C Eb G). The stretches needed to play this example make an excellent technique builder and warm up. If you want to build strength, dexterity and stamina in all your fingers, make sure you check out my book **Guitar Finger Gym**.

Example 5p – C Minor Arpeggio

In this example, I move the minor arpeggio shape between the keys of C minor and F minor.

Example 5q –Minor Arpeggio Exercise

After you have learnt the movable major and minor arpeggio shapes, play them over some backing chords. Look back at the songs mentioned on pages 47 and 48 and see if you can play arpeggios over the whole sequences. If that is too difficult at first, record a couple of chords into a looping device and use that as your backing for arpeggio practice.

7th arpeggios have a more sophisticated sound than major and minor arpeggios. Example 5r shows the movable major 7 arpeggio shape with the root note of 'C' on the 5th string.

Example 5r – C Major 7 Arpeggio

A fun way to build warm ups is to use skip-a-note patterns. In this example I use the C major 7 arpeggio (C E G B) shape but not in sequential order. This sequence warms up all the fingers, making it a very useful exercise. **Example 5s – C Major 7 Skip-a-Note Pattern**

The C Dominant 7 (C E G Bb) arpeggio is another useful shape to learn. Remember that these arpeggio shapes have no open strings so they can be moved to any key.

Example 5t – C Dominant 7 Arpeggio

Here is the skip-a-note technique builder exercise for the C Dominant 7 arpeggio shape.

Example 5u – C Dominant 7 Skip-a-Note

The final arpeggio shape to learn in is the movable minor 7th arpeggio. In example 5v I demonstrate this in 'C', creating the C minor 7th arpeggio (C Eb G Bb).

Example 5v – C Minor 7 Arpeggio

Example 5w shows the C minor 7th arpeggio using the skip-a-note pattern.

Example 5w – C Minor 7th Skip-a-Note

Scales and arpeggios form the foundation of learning any instrument. Transferring your knowledge from standard tuning will take time, but in the long run will make you a far more valuable musician and help you to create your own music.

This chapter is meant to give you the building blocks on which you can further your DADGAD scale and arpeggio development. I recommend spending 5/10 minutes a day on scales and arpeggios at the start of your warm up. This will build both discipline and fretboard fluency.

Chapter Six – Cascading Scales

I remember watching a friend play in DADGAD tuning years ago, and him making the guitar sound like a harp. I was both amazed and thoroughly intrigued at how this sound was created. Enter the beautiful world of cascading scales.

A cascading scale combines open strings and fretted notes, so that the notes can sustain over each other to create a harp-like sound. When playing a cascading scale let each note ring out into each other; this is made a lot easier by the inclusion of lots of open strings. Because each cascading scale uses open strings, they are not movable shapes, however you can apply a capo to change the key if needed.

As well as the use of open strings, you can add legato (hammer-ons and pull-offs) to a cascading scale to enhance the free-flowing sound. This is more prominent when the cascading scale shape is across two octaves.

Example 6a is a traditional fretted D Major scale across one octave. This shape will likely feel familiar in both sound and technique.

Example 6a – Fretted One Octave D Major Scale

In example 6b the notes of the D Major scale are re-arranged to create a cascading scale shape that includes many open strings.

Example 6b – Cascading One Octave D Major Scale

Often, in DADGAD you can play one scale in multiple ways. Here is the same one-octave D major cascading scale but fretted slightly differently.

Example 6c – D Major Scale One Octave Variation

Example 6d shows a fretted D Mixolydian scale across one octave.

Example 6d – Fretted One Octave D Mixolydian Scale

Here is the same D Mixolydian scale but arranged in the harp-like cascading scale format.

Example 6e – Cascading One Octave D Mixolydian Scale

Shown below is another way to fret the same one octave D Mixolydian scale.

Example 6f - Cascading One Octave D Mixolydian Scale Variation

Example 6g demonstrates a fretted D Natural Minor scale (D E F G A Bb C).

Example 6g – Fretted D Natural Minor Scale One Octave

Next is the D Natural Minor scale arranged as a one-octave cascading scale. I recommend playing the fretted version of the scale and then the cascading version after, to hear the different sounds created by the same scale.

Example 6h - Cascading D Natural Minor Scale One Octave

If playing the D Natural Minor scale with the shape shown above feels uncomfortable, then use this variation.

Example 6i - Cascading D Natural Minor Scale One Octave Variation

Now it's time to learn two-octave cascading scales in a variety of scale types and keys. This may require some work as some of the fretting can be a little uncomfortable at first, but believe me, the resulting sound is worth it. Aim to keep each note ringing into each other, and only let any fretted notes go as late as possible. The smoother the transition between the notes the better the cascading effect will sound.

Example 6j is a two-octave D major cascading scale shape. The first bar will feel familiar as you learnt it in a previous example.

Example 6j – Two Octave Cascading D Major Scale

There is only one note difference between a D Major scale (D E F# G A B **C#**) and a D Mixolydian scale (D E F# G A B **C**). The C# in D Major scale becomes a C in the D Mixolydian scale. Although it is only one note different, the sound of the Mixolydian scale is very much more bluesy than its major scale counterpart.

Example 6k - Two Octave Cascading D Mixolydian Scale

The final cascading scale in the key of D is the two-octave D Natural Minor scale.

Example 6l - Two Octave Cascading D Natural Minor Scale

As well as learning cascading scales around a central note of 'D' it is important to branch out and use them in a wide variety of keys.

The next examples demonstrate the power of adding in hammer-ons and pull-offs to help create the smooth sound of a cascading scale.

Example 6m is a two-octave F Major scale (F G A Bb C D E) arranged to include legato and open strings.

Example 6m – Two Octave Cascading F Major Scale

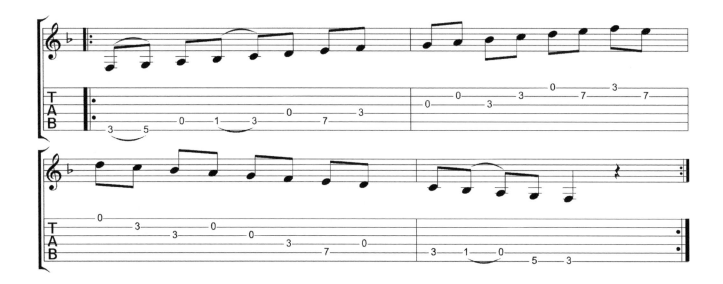

Next is a two octave cascading G Major scale.

Example 6n - Two Octave Cascading G Major Scale

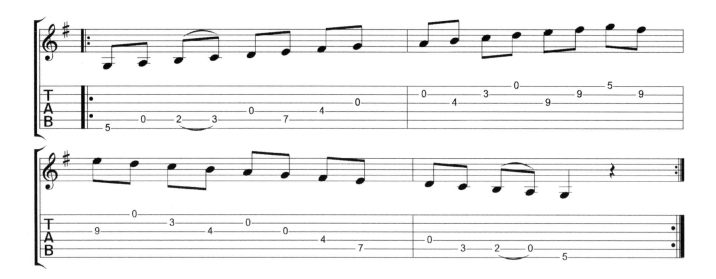

Example 6o carries on the theme of two-octave cascading scales, this time with the A Major scale (A B C# D E F# G#).

Example 6o – Two Octave Cascading A Major Scale

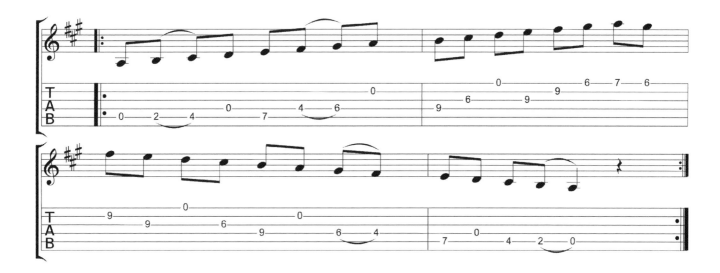

Next up is a cascading two-octave C Major scale (C D E F G A B).

Example 6p - Two Octave Cascading C Major Scale

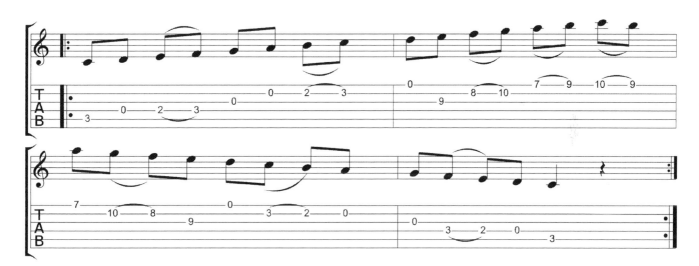

I love the tonality of the Natural Minor scale, so pairing it with the cascading technique was a real winner for me.

Example 6q displays the A Natural Minor scale (A B C D E F G) across two octaves
.

Example 6q - Two Octave Cascading A Natural Minor Scale

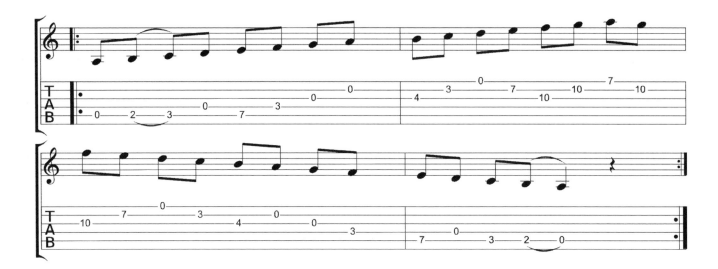

Next is the cascading G Natural Minor scale (G A Bb C D Eb F) across two octaves.

Example 6r - Two Octave Cascading G Natural Minor Scale

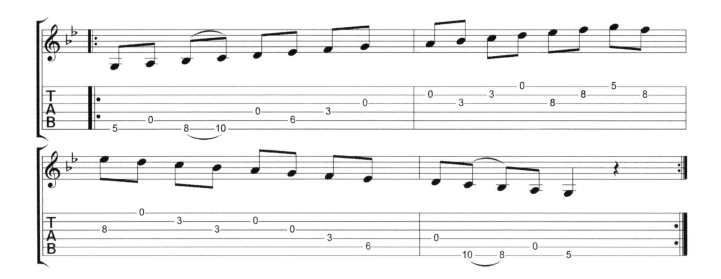

The piece I wrote for this chapter is entitled 'Droney'. It uses the A Natural Minor scale arranged as a cascading scale for the majority of the main theme, but at the end migrates to the D Natural Minor scale.

I had so much fun writing this piece and this chapter in general; never had playing a scale felt so fresh, fun and original as applying cascading scales across the fretboard. Use the scales in this chapter as your starting point to write pieces similar to 'Droney'.

I love hearing pieces that my students have created, so if you have written any pieces in DADGAD since reading this book, I would love to hear them. My email address is in the conclusion.

Example 6s – Droney

Droney

Cascading scales are one of the main attractions of DADGAD tuning. Although they are possible in standard tuning, DADGAD allows for much easier and wider access to this stunning technique. The drawback with using cascading scales is that you can be restricted to individual keys and scale types due to the difficulty in fretting the notes. The cascading scales shown in this chapter offer a few fundamental scale types for you to start with, and I recommend learning these scales in depth before pursuing other cascading scales.

In general, cascading scales tend to suit seven-note scales instead of pentatonic (five-note) and hexatonic (six-note) scales. However, it is possible to fret a broad range of scales using this technique.

Remember that if you love the sound of a specific cascading scale but want to move it into a different key, a capo easily moves the notes to the key you require. I am a long-time advocate of Kyser capos, and would highly recommend investing in a decent capo. Remember: 'buy cheap, buy twice'.

I had so much fun using cascading scales, as they brought me away from the traditional scale shapes and sounds. As well as learning the examples written throughout this chapter, aim to write new licks using the cascading scales as soon as you feel comfortable using them. Be sure to document your ideas by filming them, recording the audio or simply writing them down in notation or tab.

Chapter Seven – DADGAD Specialities

There are certain things you can do in DADGAD that are not possible in standard tuning. Every tuning has its own unique structure allowing for patterns, shapes and techniques that are exclusive to it. In this chapter, I am going to show you how to play one-finger power chords, natural harmonics, octaves and creative chord voicings.

Understanding the power DADGAD is half the battle. Once mastered, you can write music with these techniques and open up a whole new world of creativity.

In DADGAD (or even just drop D, DADGBE) you can play a power chord with just one finger. Example 7a shows the D Minor Pentatonic scale using the power chord shape. I recommend using your first finger to fret these mini-barre power chords.

Power Chords

Example 7a – D Minor Pentatonic Power Chords

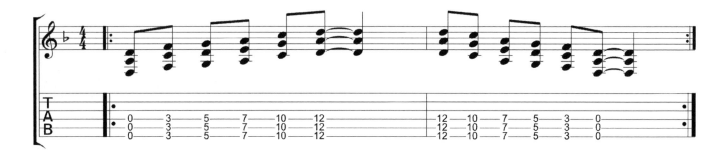

DADGAD can rock! Example 7b uses the D Minor Pentatonic scale from the previous example with some slides and syncopation to create a powerful modern sounding rock riff.

Example 7b – D Minor Pentatonic Rock Riff

The next example is the D Blues scale (D F G Ab A C) constructed using power chord shapes on the 6th, 5th and 4th strings.

Example 7c – D Blues Scale Power Chords

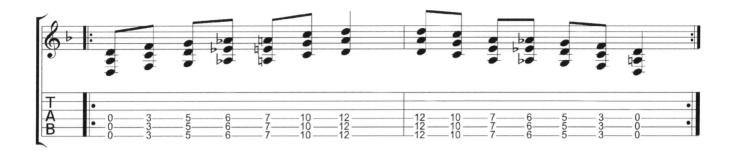

Example 7d combines the D Blues scale with palm mutes to create a heavier rock metal sound reminiscent of bands like Avenged Sevenfold.

Example 7d

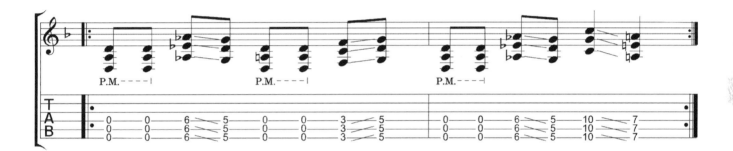

Example 7e demonstrates the D Major scale using power chord shapes.

Example 7e – D Major Scale Power Chords

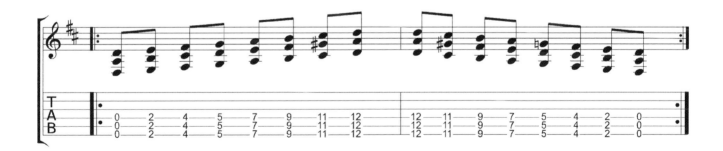

A variation on strumming the whole power chord shape at once is to pick the notes of the power chord individually. Example 7f arpeggiates the power chords shapes based around the D Major scale.

Example 7f – Major Power Chords

Example 7g is the D Mixolydian scale played using power chord shapes.

Example 7g – D Mixolydian Scale Power Chords

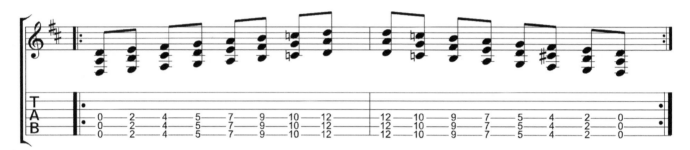

The Mixolydian scale works brilliantly in Blues and Rock music. As well as learning the examples shown here, create your own and adapt them to suit your own playing style.

Example 7h – D Mixolydian Power Chord Riff

The final power chord scale in this chapter is the D Natural Minor scale.

Example 7i – D Natural Minor Power Chord Scale

The final power chord idea combines the D Natural Minor scale with a busy rhythmic pattern. Listen to how I phrase this example on the accompanying audio track.

Example 7j – Natural Minor Power Chord Riff

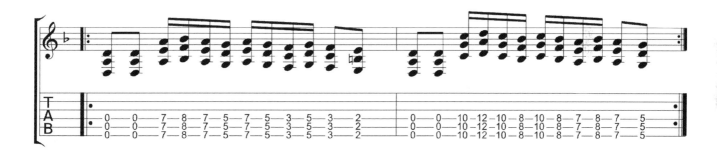

Natural Harmonics

Natural harmonics are of course possible in standard tuning, however in DADGAD they can become a really powerful addition to your technique arsenal. Sometimes getting a natural harmonic to ring properly is a little tricky, so make sure you are using new strings and touch the string incredibly lightly directly above the fret.

Watch this video I filmed on natural harmonics to help you learn how to properly fret and play them. **http://www.fundamental-changes.com/natural-harmonics-dadgad-video-guitar-lesson/**

Also, for a more information and a great series on producing natural harmonics, check out these lessons on **www.fundamental-changes.com**.

http://www.fundamental-changes.com/harmonics-on-guitar/

Don't forget, all lessons on Fundamental-Changes.com are searchable by name.

There are many places where a natural harmonic can be played and Example 7k shows natural harmonics at the 12th frets across all six strings.

Example 7k – 12th Fret Natural Harmonics

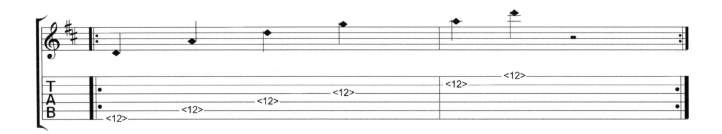

Example 7l combines the 6th string note of 'D' with some natural 12th fret harmonics.

Example 7l – Drone and 12th Fret Harmonics

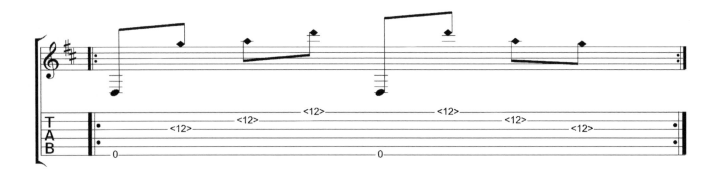

Natural harmonics situated around the 7th frets are also commonly used.

Example 7m

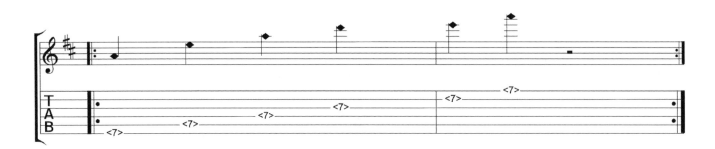

Here is a 'call and response' between a bassline and some natural harmonics at the 7th fret. Getting used to fretting standard notes and natural harmonics within the same bar will require some practice, but the sound it creates is worth the extra effort.

Example 7n

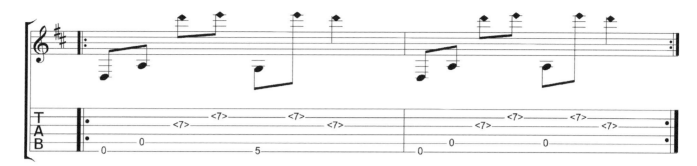

The 5th fret is another common place to fret natural harmonics.

Example 7o

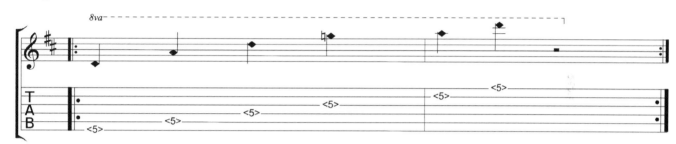

Example 7p uses a D major chord progression but ends each bar with a 5th fret natural harmonic. Some of the pieces featured later on in this book use this technique extensively, so dedicated practice now will save a lot of work later on.

Example 7p

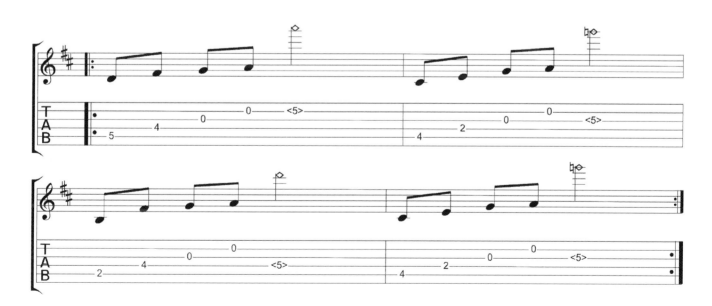

Octaves

Octaves are far easier to achieve in DADGAD than in standard tuning and are a useful compositional tool for writing riffs and songs. Due to the nature of DADGAD tuning, the octave shapes remain consistent throughout all the string sets, allowing for ease of use and speed of learning. Once you have learnt the octave shapes, aim to create a mini riff or idea using each new shape.

Example 7q is the D Major scale using an octave pattern on the 6th and 4th strings.

Example 7q – D Major Scale in Octaves

The next example shows the A Blues scale in octaves using the 5th and 2nd strings.

Example 7r – A Blues Scale in Octaves

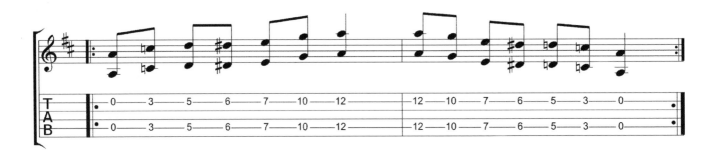

Example 7s shows the D Mixolydian scale in octaves on the 4th and 2nd strings.

Example 7s – D Mixolydian in Octaves

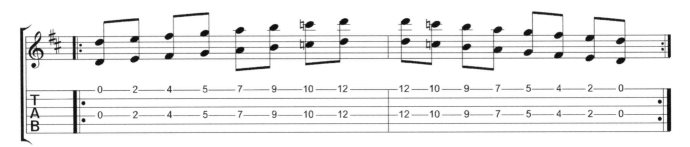

Here is the D Mixolydian scale in a two-octave pattern that spans across all the different string set patterns (6+4, 5+2 and 4+1).

Example 7t

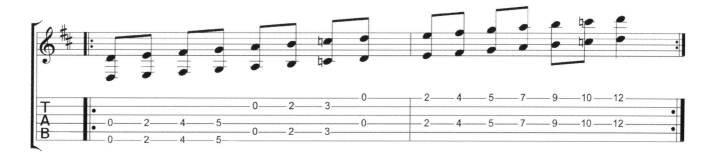

Now that you have learnt how to apply octave scale patterns in DADGAD, it is time to use them in a musical context. Example 7u uses the D Mixolydian scale in a simple bluesy octave pattern. You can either fingerpick this pattern or use hybrid picking (pick and fingers). If you want a detailed way to learn to hybrid pick, be sure to check out my book **Melodic Rock Soloing For Guitar**.

Example 7u – D Mixolydian with bass note

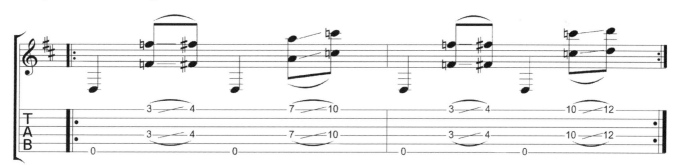

'Got Blues?' is a four bar blues riff that once again utilises the D Mixolydian scale. I recommend learning this idea in very small blocks of a few notes at a time and building each block together slowly with a metronome. The hammer-ons, pull-offs and slides between octave shapes help bring them 'to life' and are well worth incorporating into your own DADGAD octave ideas.

Example 7v – Got Blues?

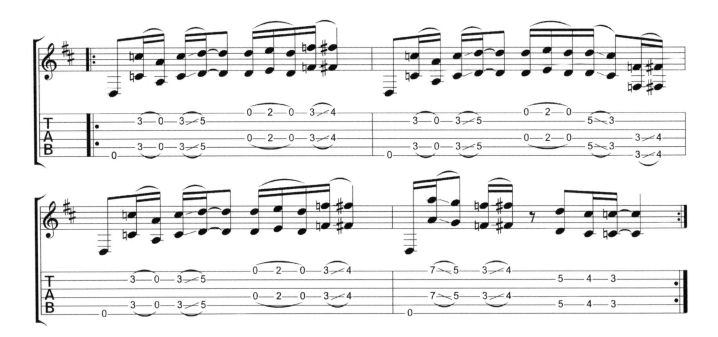

Creative Chord Voicings

With DADGAD tuning, we have the ability to create interesting and sometimes unusual chord voicings that would be impossible (or at least extremely difficult) in standard tuning. The next few examples demonstrate some of my favourite DADGAD chord voicings. If you fancy a challenge, I have left each chord nameless for you to work out the root notes and then use the chord type to name the chord. See the appendix at the back for the chord names.

Example 7w features a close 'sus2' voicing, that has a modern, hip sound. Name this chord by using the 3rd string 'G' as the root note, for example, the first chord would be 'Gsus2'.

Example 7w – Hip 'sus2' Chord Voicing

Example 7x shows another cool jazzy voicing that would be extremely difficult to play in standard tuning. This is a major7sus4 shape where the root is defined by the note on the 'D' string. For example, the first chord is a Gmaj7sus4 because the note on the 4th string is a 'G'. Name the others in this sequence by working out their root notes on the 'D' string. Check the appendix for the answers!

Example 7x – Major7sus4 Chord Voicing

Example 7y uses some 5 and 6 string '6/9' chords. You can name these chords from the 5th string root note, for example, the first chord is a D6/9.

Example 7y – 6/9 Shape

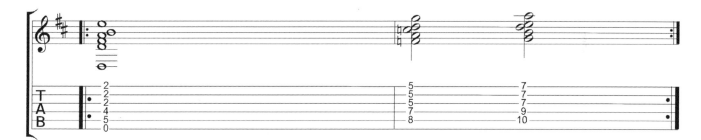

Example 7z arpeggiates the chords learnt in the previous example.

Example 7z – 6/9 Arpeggios

To finish this chapter, I have written two pieces for you to learn. The first piece 'Harmonik' combines ringing chord shapes with natural harmonics and finishes with a lovely D Natural Minor cascading scale run. Listen to how I play these pieces with the accompanying audio track. This piece revolves around three chords of D minor 9, C5 and Bbmaj7, shown below.

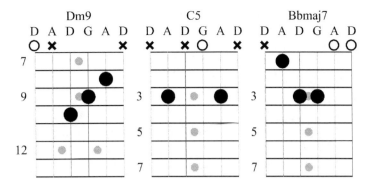

Example 7za – Harmonik

Harmonik

The final example in this chapter is called 'Droney'. This piece is based on the chord voicings that you learnt earlier on and is put together to form an ultra-modern jazz fusion example. This is one of my favourite songs that I wrote for this book. I believe it's original and shows my personal sound.

Example 7zb – Droney

Droney

Chapter Eight – One Day

I am lucky to be able to include two pieces in this book by my close friend and DADGAD master Neale McGinn. One Day has a laid back happy feel centered around a catchy melody. It is a fingerpicking piece, but you can experiment with hybrid picking (pick and fingers) if that feels more comfortable.

One Day is based on the D Major Scale, giving it a happy and cheerful vibe. Learn this piece just one bar at a time, slowly and with a metronome. This track was played 'free time' to allow for subtle nuances that help give it its feel, but I recommend starting at around 60 beats a minute when you are practicing each bar.

Before you dive straight into the full piece, I want to explain a technique that Neale uses in the final two bars. Neale creates an artificial harmonic (labeled A.H in the notation) by fretting the 2nd fret of the high 'D' string but lightly touching the 14th fret of the same string (an octave above) with his first finger on his picking hand. This creates an artificial harmonic an octave above the original F# note. Example 8a demonstrates the final two bars of this piece which include this artificial harmonic sound.

This technique was made famous by the acoustic maestro Tommy Emmanuel and can be used on multiple strings to create a waterfall harmonic sound. Watch his rendition of the song Somewhere Over The Rainbow to see this in action. **https://www.youtube.com/watch?v=0cHeNscKZN0**

Example 8a – Artificial Harmonic

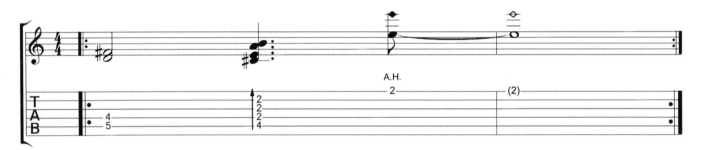

Now you have grasped how an artificial harmonic is created, it is time to check out the full piece. If you get stuck on a particular bar or phrase, use a different fingering. Often just by changing one finger within a pattern you can feel much more at ease with what you are playing. Throughout this book, you will notice that within the pieces I have not included the chord names in the full transcriptions. This is done on purpose so you learn the chord shapes first, and see how they fit into each piece.

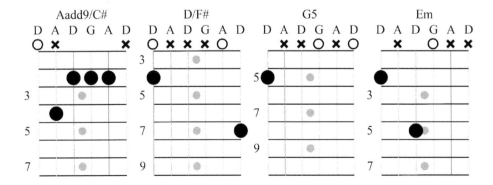

One Day

As well as listening to Neale's wonderful performance of this track, I have included a slowed down midi version, so you can play along at a slower tempo.

Chapter Nine – Sasha

My incredible cocker spaniel Sasha, brings me joy and happiness every single day. When I was writing this book, I was out walking her and saw the pure joy she got from just rolling around in the middle of the park. That single moment was the inspiration for this piece of music and helped shape every note and phrase into what it has become today.

'Sasha' incorporates lots of techniques and strategies that you have learnt throughout this book. Cascading scales and natural harmonics are two main focal points to this piece, and help give it its fluid sound.

The next examples are small extracts from the full piece, to help you to understand how it was created. Example 9a is the D Major scale (in the cascading scale format and ends with a double-stop natural harmonic.

Example 9a – Cascading D Major Scale and Natural Harmonics

Throughout this track, I blend finger picked-chords with natural harmonics. This is a very common technique among DADGAD fingerstyle players.

Example 9b – Blending Chords and Harmonics

Example 9c shows another fingerpicked pattern that is blended with natural harmonics, this time at the 7th fret.

Example 9c – Chords and Harmonics 2

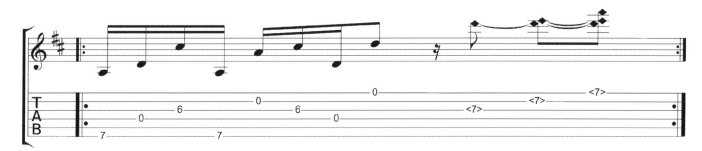

The outro again uses a repeating cascading D Major scale pattern. I have included directions showing how I fingerpick this underneath the notation, but feel free to play this phrase in any way that feels comfortable.

Example 9d – Cascading Outro

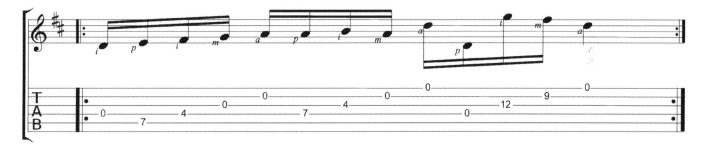

Now that I have broken down specific bars of the piece, it is time to look at the full track. As well as learning Sasha as a whole piece, make sure you 'steal' chord shapes, cascading scale runs and natural harmonic licks to build up your DADGAD lick arsenal. Remember when it comes to learning music you can never 'steal' enough from other players!

As well as listening to my performance of this track, I have included a slowed down midi version of this piece, so you can play along at a slower tempo.

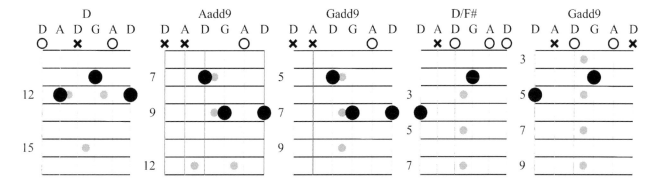

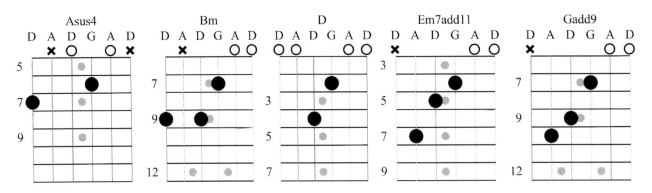

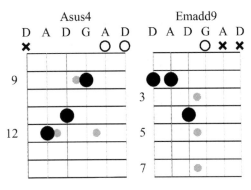

Example 9e – Sasha Full Piece

Sasha

Chapter Ten – Gone Pickin'

Gone Pickin' is a fusion of country, bluegrass, jazz and funk. For a different approach, I based this track around using a pick, instead of the more traditional DADGAD fingerstyle.

This track is based around the D Mixolydian scale to give it a more bluesy flavour than the previous Major-scale pieces. I highly recommend spending time learning the small bite-size examples below before attempting the full song.

Example 10a is the introduction to the track and uses a repetitive legato (hammer-on) pattern across multiple strings. The challenge here is the stretch between the 4th and 7th frets using the first and fourth fingers. If you are having trouble with dexterity or stamina in any of your fingers, I recommend my book **Guitar Finger Gym** which can help guide you to a more efficient practice regime.

I have included the picking directions that I used in the notation but in general stick to strict alternate picking (down, up) where possible.

Example 10a – Hammer-ons

Example 10b is a D Mixolydian riff that spells out the notes of a D7 (D F# A C) chord. I would advise you to omit the muted notes at first to focus on the riff and groove before including adding them back in. Listen to the audio track a few times to hear how I phrase this example.

Example 10b – Funky D Mixolydian

Cross-string picking is a challenge, especially when there is a string skip involved, but once you have learnt the picking for example 10c it repeats for four bars of the song. Keep the pull-off both dynamically and rhythmically identical to the other notes. Although I play this track at around 125 beats per minute, start off around 60/70 beats per minute when you are learning each example.

Example 10c – Cross String Picking

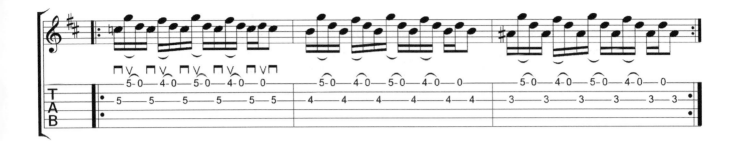

For the final lick of the piece, I wanted to write something memorable and a bit more challenging. What I came up with sounds like Nuno Bettencourt (Extreme) playing a jazz line. Its syncopation mixed with chromaticism and articulations make for my favourite example in this book.

This lick works well over a D7 chord and uses the D Blues scale (D F G Ab A C) and D Mixolydian scale (D E F# G A B C#) with some chromatic passing notes to add colour.

Example 10d – Jazzy Nuno Bettencourt

Example 10e – Gone Pickin' Full Piece

I always tell my students to **play the guitar with their brains and ears, not their eyes and hands.** What I mean is that your ear should always be your guide so that they don't rely on specific finger patterns and movements to play music. Before you start this piece, I would like you to listen through to the track through headphones at least twice to hear all its performance.

Gone Pickin' is a fairly technical track so I have included picking and strumming articulations as a guide. I have also included a slowed down midi version of this piece, so you can hear it played at a slower tempo as well.

Gone Pickin'

Chapter Eleven – 4 For Blues

In this final chapter, I will dissect Neale's piece 4 For Blues. There is a wealth of licks, riffs and lines you can steal from this track and I am sure it will be a piece you will revisit for many years to come.

4 For Blues is in D minor, and uses a variety of scales but centres around the D Blues scale. I have broken down the track for you to learn as bite-size examples, so that when you learn the full piece it will feel much less daunting.

Example 11a is a superb D Blues scale lick that Neale uses at the end of different sections within the piece. You will notice that this scale is arranged in a cascading scale pattern and uses legato (hammer-ons and pull-offs) to create the smooth flowing sound. This lick is a real winner, and one to add to your DADGAD arsenal.

Example 11a – D Blues Scale Lick

Double-stops (two notes played at the same time) are a brilliant addition to a guitarists rhythm and lead playing skills. Example 11b shows a D Natural Minor scale (D E F G A Bb C) ascending in double-stops on the 2nd and 1st strings.

Example 11b – D Minor Double Stops Ascending

Example 11c shows the D Natural Minor scale (D E F G A Bb C) descending on the 2nd and 1st strings.

Example 11c - D Minor Double Stops Descending

By adding a bend to a double-stop, you can create a very bluesy sound. Example 11d shows how to add a semitone bend on the 2nd string while holding a note on the 1st string.

Example 11d – Double-Stops with Bends

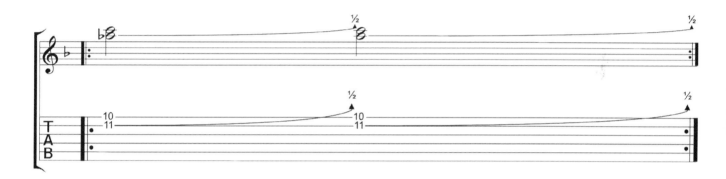

Now you can add a droning 'D' root note to the double-stop bends seen in the previous example.

Example 11e – Bass Note and Double-Stop Bends

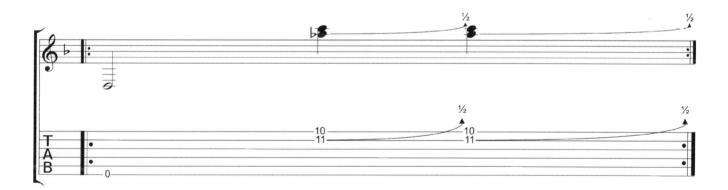

Example 11f mixes a double-stop bend, with three other double-stop shapes on 2nd and 1st strings.

Example 11f – Moving Double Stop Shapes

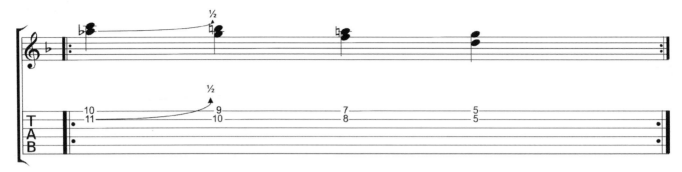

The main theme in 4 for Blues revolves around bass notes that jump between the 6th and 4th strings. Before adding the double-stop, get used to using your thumb to pick between the bass notes. Try to see this example as both a bass note pattern and a double-stop bending pattern.

Example 11g – Alternate Bass Notes

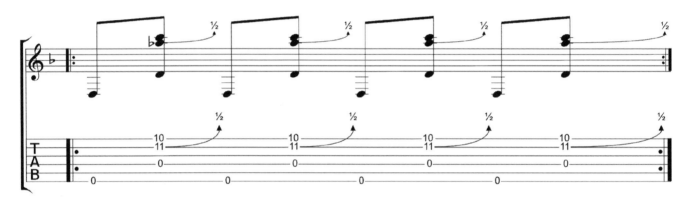

The next mini fingerpicking workout involves alternating bass notes and two different double-stop shapes, one with a bend and one without.

Example 11h – Alternate bass and double-stops

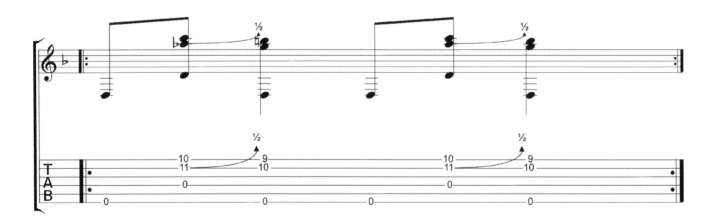

Now that you have cracked the fundamental building blocks of bass notes and double-stops, you can look at the first bar of the main theme. I played example 11i very straight with a metronome as this is the best way to practice it. When you can play it fluently, you can copy the incredible feel that Neale uses in the track.

Example 11i

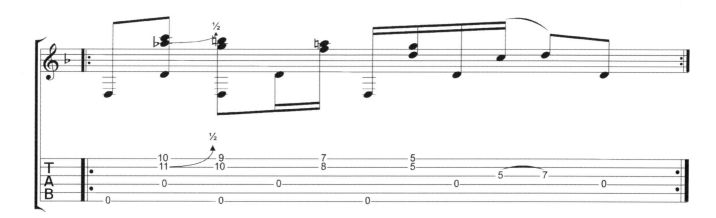

Example 11j is bar two of the central theme used in 4 For Blues. The lovely 12th fret natural harmonic at the end of the bar is a real highlight.

Example 11j

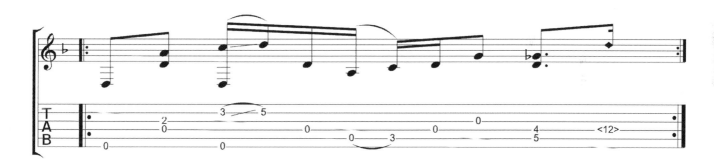

When you have completed the last two examples, you can put them together in a two bar phrase.

Example 11k

The final lick to learn before diving into the full track is the two bar lick used in the breakdown. This lick uses lots of octave patterns (see Chapter Seven for more details) and has a percussive blues sound. As always, start off extremely slowly with a metronome set at around 60 beats per minute, and only increase the speed when you can play the lick five times correctly in a row.

Example 11l – Breakdown Section

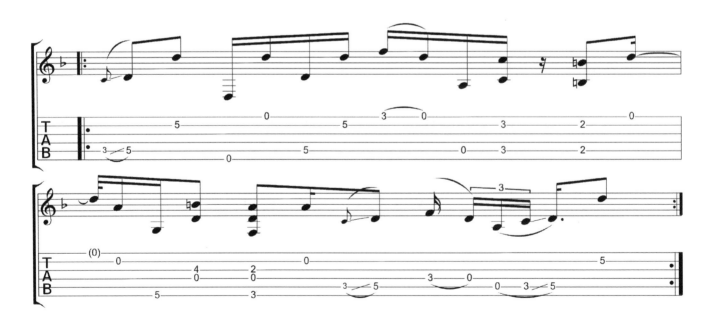

If you have worked sequentially through this chapter, this track will seem a lot less intimidating. My advice is to listen through to the attached audio track several times, and follow along with the piece to see how Neale phrases every lick. The more familiar you can become with how the tune sounds, the easier it will be to know if you are playing it correctly. As with the other pieces in this book, I have included a slowed down midi track for you to play along to when learning 4 for Blues.

Neale uses lots of mutes (labeled P.M) and artificial harmonics (labeled A.H) throughout the piece. I recommend learning this piece without these articulation at first to get used to how to fret each phrase before adding them back in.

For all the tunes featured throughout this book I recommend the following:

- Learn the pieces fully.

- Steal individual licks and phrases.

- Write your own track based on the licks you have 'stolen'.

- Keep coming back to the pieces and aim to see new chord shapes, licks and phrases you didn't see previously.

- Play them with other musicians (or with yourself on a looping device or recorded track).

- Have fun.

Example 11m – 4 For Blues Full Piece

4 For Blues

Congratulations! You made it! I hope you have discovered a wealth of new ideas for playing in DADGAD tuning and that you can keep coming back to year after year. Like everything with guitar playing, DADGAD does require work but as I always say 'The more time you devote to playing your guitar, the better friend it will be'.

Conclusion

Whether you are just beginning your journey, or you are an experienced DADGAD player, everyone can benefit by adding in new techniques and ideas. Use the examples in this book as a starting point for creating musical lines, phrases and complete songs. Let your ears guide you, and don't rely on the finger patterns and scale shapes that you know to be the 'safe' notes. Remember the saying "If it sounds good it is, if it sounds bad….it probably is too".

Practice what you don't know, not what you do! - This is quite simply the best advice I can give any musician.

An important musical goal should be to play with other people, so while you are developing your skills in this book find time to jam with other musicians. Playing with other instrumentalists is the best way to improve your musicianship.

If you want further ideas to improve your guitar playing check out my other books **Finger Guitar Gym**, **Melodic Rock Soloing For Guitar** and **Exotic Pentatonic Soloing For Guitar**, which are also available through **www.Fundamental-Changes.com**

My passion in life is teaching people to play and express themselves through the guitar. If you have any questions, please get in touch and I will do my best to respond as quickly as possible.

You can contact me on **simeypratt@gmail.com** or via the **Fundamental Changes YouTube channel**.

Song Discography

Here are a selection of some wonderful DADGAD tunes for you to learn; some require a capo to perform in the original key.

Led Zeppelin – Black Mountain Side, White Summer

Martin Simpson – Long Distance Love

Rory Gallagher – Out On The Western Plain

Stephen Stills – Treetop Flier

Pierre Bensusan – Nice Feeling / Salsa / (Almost all his work)

Bert Jansch - Blackwaterside

Laurence Juber – While My Guitar Gently Weeps / Every Breath You Take

Michael Hedges – Ragamuffin

Peppino D'Agostino – Echo Of Delphi Valley

Andy Mckee – Into The Ocean

Daniele Bazzani – DADGAD

The Stone Roses – Love Spreads

Fionn Regan – Abacus

Iron And Wine – Half Moon

David Ryan Harris – Turn Around

Stuart Ryan – Albatross

Eric Roche – Smells Like Teen Spirit

Other Books from Fundamental Changes

Facebook: FundamentalChangesInGuitar

Appendix

For your reference I have included two DADGAD fretboard neck diagrams, one without #'s and b's and one with every note on the fretboard.

DADGAD Fretboard – No #'s or b's

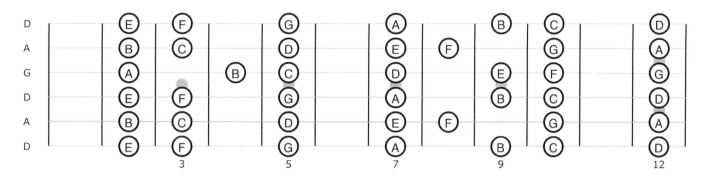

DADGAD Fretboard – All Notes

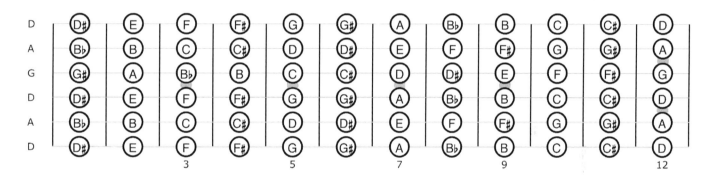

Answers to Chord Names

Throughout the book I left certain examples without chord names so you could try to name them.

Example 4d – F major (bar 1) and G major (bar 2)

Example 4s – Dm7 (bar 1 +3), Gm7, Abm7, Am7 (bar 2 and 4), Bbmaj7, Am7 (bar 5), Gm7 (bar 7), Bbmaj7, C7 (bar 8).

Example 7w – Gsus2, Asus2, Bsus2, Csus2, Dsus2, Esus2, Fsus2, Gsus2

Example 7x – Gmaj7sus4, Amaj7sus4, Bmaj7sus4, Cmaj7sus4

Example 7y – D6/9, F6/9, G6/9

39376334R00065

Made in the USA
San Bernardino, CA
25 September 2016